LIFE MASTERY

A SELF-ESTEEM HANDBOOK
FOR ADULTS AND CHILDREN

LIFE MASTERY
A SELF-ESTEEM HANDBOOK
FOR ADULTS AND CHILDREN

BY CLAUDIA KING

LIGHT PATHS COMMUNICATIONS

LIFE MASTERY:
A SELF-ESTEEM HANDBOOK
FOR ADULTS AND CHILDREN

A practical guide to self-discovery which supports and
nurtures positive self-esteem.

By Claudia King © 1993

Cover design by Dave Sisk © 1994

Book layout by Carey Wilson

LIGHT PATHS COMMUNICATIONS
P.O. Box 3576
Chico, CA 95927

ISBN 0 9639401 0 4

CONTENTS

LIST OF ILLUSTRATIONS

FOREWORD

All that I have been and known has led me here. These acknowledgements are a portion of the experiences and relationships for which I am grateful. First I thank my family, my mother, Thelma King, and daughters, Kia and Kendra McLean, and five grandchildren, Nicholas, Ian, Roxanne, Elijah, and Nora. Like many people who are committed to growth and enlightenment my family experience has been my foundation and focus for healing. How can any of us know what our own part in growth processes is — as if we could extract our presence from these relationships, and study it as an isolated thing? I also thank long time friends John Zalais, Lynn Good, Donna Galassi, and Lina Shanklin for their loving support over the years. For the courage of my fire walk teacher, Terry Downey, I am grateful. I wish to acknowledge my spiritual community which is large. In particular I am grateful for the support and friendship of Cherie and Bob Pollock, Lorna McMurray, Marco Negrao, and Marianne Williamson. I thank my editor, Elizabeth Rhudy, layout artist Carey Wilson, cover designer David Sisk, and Griffin Printing. I am indebted to all of the teachers and principals with whom or for whom I have worked. Special thanks to the hundreds and thousands of children whom I love deeply and whose behaviors have sometimes exasperated me and pressed me to continue growing and healing.

Claudia King 1994

1. INTRODUCTION

When I arrived at college, having been co-valedictorian of my high school graduating class, the concept of "self-esteem" was not of interest to teachers or parents alike. Everyone assumed that I had high "self-esteem." I was hard-working, had never been "in trouble," and had a strong drive to succeed. Life since then has brought many reverses and painful experiences that taught me the value of a foundation of positive self-regard.

At 18 years of age I had what would be now termed "poor self-esteem." The good grades and achievements of school had given me what little sense of accomplishment my experience of a hypercritical and perfectionist society would allow. There was no conspiracy behind comparing a child to some unattainable ideal person. It was part of a process that has been going on in society for generations.

Yet today we have the insight and capacity to stop eroding children's self-esteem. While growing up I learned very little of my own inner strength, which would have taken me through the vicissitudes of life. I had to learn it at the school of hard knocks, with my children paying the price of admission. This book is presented with the intent that, out of all of the hours dedicated to teaching children intellectual skills and caring for children's physical needs, we can take time to support them in growing and developing emotionally so that they can use these skills as part of a sustained and evolving awareness. Instead of moving from one compulsive level of addictive and dysfunctional relationship to another, they can learn to develop fulfilling lives of conscious commitment to peace and harmony with one another and the environment around them. We need to help our children learn to fly and not to crash and burn.

SELF-ESTEEM

The concept of "self-esteem" refers to a gestalt or state of inner awareness. When children are very young, and when they have not been severely abused they have an unconditional acceptance of their right to be here and their positive value to life around them. They understand that their purpose is to be happy. Infants and very small children radiate a quality of love and self-acceptance which draws life and interest toward them. They are "naturally" attractive. Without sophisticated understandings of cause and effect or subtle differentiation between themselves and others, the very young have a basic foundation of self esteem or positive self-regard. This stays with the child throughout life, but becomes buried by the process of socialization. That is, children can be systematically taught that they are not worthy or of value to those around them or to themselves. Too frequently the process of teaching children that they are valueless starts early in life and continues without respite. Thus, studies show a steady deterioration in positive self-regard among children, accelerating as they move through school.

All of the exercises in this text are designed so that, given a goal of enhancing positive self-regard, they can be used to help a child become part of society and retain high self-esteem. The exercises will help the children retain contact with that part of them that naturally and essentially understands that they do have value, they do have a right to be here, — a right equal to the right of any other person or living being. In the process of teaching them about the presidents of the United States, we must also teach them that their value to the world is just as important as that of any president.

The way to strengthen the link to that inner strength is to maintain continuous self-awareness and self-acceptance. Utilizing the exercises, we adults can facilitate progressive capacity to be aware as we develop and our children grow. We cannot teach self-esteem to our children if our development in this direction has ceased. We will teach self-esteem, naturally, as it springs from our own inner-strength unfolding from growing inner-awareness.

INNER-AWARENESS AND LIFE MASTERY

Inner-awareness is such a vast world of experiences, dwarfing our knowledge of the world outside. It has been partially explored in some generalities by psychologists. But each of us has our own unique inner kingdom of feelings, knowledge, understandings, bodily information, and thoughts. This whole personal world is not simply the collection of what we learned in school but contains our basic understandings and acceptance of the universe in every cell and every vibration of the energy of our lives. We can be masters of our own being, as we can be masters of nothing else in this world. No one person can truly know another's inner world. Nor do we have the right to invalidate another's inner processes, given the fact that we have no basis from which to judge it. Another person makes decisions and behaves often as a result of a whole personal history different from our own. If we could truly see how this works, as we can when we study ourselves, we would have the greatest compassion for the dignity and the love that brings each human to every day of life.

Because self-esteem is natural, there should be very little adults need to do to allow children's self-esteem to mature and grow as they grow. However as we see a steady decline in a child's sense of positive self-conception as they move toward adulthood, we must suspect that there is much that adults do that erodes a child's sense of worthiness. There is much about society and contemporary life that is counter to a healthy self-concept. It is unlikely that this will change radically in the near future. Thus we need to start including children in processes that reverse negative self-images.

Furthermore, if positive self-regard is natural then it must be an intrinsic trait, not dependent upon anything a child learns about the world outside. The process that strengthens a sense of worth is one that has to do with a child or an adult coming to understand their inner being. Many may consider this a selfish or narcissistic quest, while considering the pursuit of all sorts of automobiles and real estate and other objects as a non-self-centered quest. It is not necessary to wait until we are middle-aged or older for self-understanding to mature. Educators need to learn to draw a perspective from children in which they can see, study and appreciate themselves, a perspective that has nothing to do with reading, writing, arithmetic, or grades.

Try this exercise as an self-introduction. It is possible to simplify the exercise for verbal children, over five years of age.

1. CONVERSATIONAL SELF-AWARENESS

For adults or children: Notice your emotional state and any sensations or feelings in your body at this moment. Notice changes in your body and emotions when you are in a debate or discussion with another person in which your beliefs or opinions are seriously questioned, perhaps even considered stupid or wrong. Do you defend yourself and your beliefs? Do you justify yourself and how you came to these opinions? Do you feel areas of tightness or pressure within your body? Do you feel uncertain? Do you experience a change of mood, anger, fear, sadness...? Does your mind flail about wildly looking for ways to get even or to show this other person what's wrong with him? Do you begin to think of all sorts of flaws that the other person has in body, personality, lifestyle? Are there some subjects to which you react strongly when your opinions are challenged? Are there subjects about which you do not care whether someone else disagrees with you? Simply observe this about yourself.

As you learn to watch yourself, you may begin to see patterns in what you think and how you respond to others. Noticing patterns is part of the process of knowing who we are. All of us know ourselves to a degree and probably believe that we have good and bad qualities of character or personality. Patterns are clues to why we act as we do. Patterns can become fixed to defend ourselves against changes that we do not like. Fixed patterns do not allow for new or better ways of living and solving problems. Patterns change as we become conscious of them.

THE COST OF POOR SELF-ESTEEM

Now let us look at the terrible cost that ignoring self-esteem has extracted from our society. Those problems directly related to self-esteem problems would include: addictions such as alcohol and drugs, gang activity, child and teenage suicide, school dropout rates, runaway children, teenage pregnancies, child and spousal abuse, divorce, and so forth. While it may take many years to turn these trends and issues around, programs that continuously and systematically focus upon self-esteem for both adults and children can impact the social costs of this partial list of problems.

GROUND OF BEING

Our life is like a river and in no two instances are we the same. Yet the ground of our being, our very foundation or basis, in which our self esteem rests, remains constant. Our ground of being is layered over with memories that render self-images, — images as a child, as an adolescent, as an adult. The images are set into every part of mind and body, minute by minute. Thus we can choose the images through which our consciousness passes to reach our essence. We can remember (imagine) our past from the point of view of love and compassion, or from our fears and regrets. If we remain angry and unforgiving about things we feel were wrong in our past we will duplicate the pain and suffering they brought us by continually returning to those images of ourselves. If we wish to connect with the deepest quiet at the core of our being, our memories will be colored with joy and forgiveness. We can learn to trust a process of releasing painful images and moving beyond to a ground of being that contains all possibilities. As we learn to let this quiet essence guide us we can regain our initial ability to live more natural, less stress-filled lives. We can choose between quiet and peace or suffering and illness. For this inner essence is the repository of the natural healthy vitality and glow we had as infants, when we were in continuous and spontaneous contact with it. It is still there.

LAYERS OF THOUGHT AND CONSCIOUSNESS

I will briefly touch on how our ground of positive self-esteem fits into the layers of our consciousness. We are constantly acting and expressing from the very deepest parts of our mind. We act and form beliefs from the parts of the mind that do not necessarily seem to form rational groupings of ideas at this moment. For instance, I experienced being shamed about failing while growing up. Now, although I may have forgotten the exact experiences and feelings they engendered, when I feel I am about to fail my mind goes into a panic. Sometimes it even goes blank. I am so accustomed to this happening that I think it is normal. I have developed rationalizations (beliefs) about why I feel so anxious about success. Our unconscious as well as conscious thoughts are are accessing memories of all of our experiences. A flow of information is brought to the surface of our minds in response to what is going on in our lives. Our consciousness stores information about suffering and reactions to negative experiences and feelings. If we persist in drawing upon our store of negative, upsetting, disappointing thoughts and experiences we will bring them forward to fill our surface mental patterns. Our negative sequencing can lead to all manner of self-destructive behavior. In my example of feeling shame about failure, I can stop bringing the shame forward by becoming aware of it. Rather than rushing forward in the grip of panic, denial and defensiveness, and attendant unconscious behavioral patterns such as working even harder, I can notice that each time I think I might fail the same series of thoughts and behaviors emerge. Instead of unconscious reaction, I can choose to tell myself that I am a successful and loving person regardless of outward evidence. My self-talk slowly diminishes the power of the shame.

MASTERY

Our minds also retain all positive experiences, feelings, and thoughts. Out of the deep parts of our mind come inspiration, intuition, sudden insights, and breakthroughs. The latter are the source of greatness in the arts and sciences. Included in our essential mental basis is the intelligence of the universe. It is a deep cellular intelligence which turns embryo into babies, babies into children, children into adults. It guides a downhill skier moving at 100 miles an hour past rocks and stones. It is also the source of the love that sustains our bodies and our lives. In the positive qualities of our consciousness, which are our permanent human heritage, rest our capacity to revitalize our lives moment by moment, to bring back a full realization of positive self-valuation to any human.

True mastery occurs when our knowledge of ourselves is sufficient to sustain us through periods when our mastery of professions, relationships, and survival seem in question. When we are in continuous contact with our ground of being we have a calm and self-assured attitude. We see that problems posed by these changes offer us exciting opportunities to learn and grow.

THOUGHTS AND SELF-AWARENESS

Notice how your thoughts are continuously changing. The roots of our self-esteem do not change. But our mind's contact with passing thoughts is affected by layers of fear and anxiety. We create consciousness layers based in our attempts to master the world. Mastery can be deeply rooted by recognizing and experiencing ourselves as an expression of our essence, moment by moment. Or mastery can be a surface pattern of thoughts, concepts, and beliefs that allow mastery of a profession or activity. One moment we feel we know everything necessary for the mastery of that profession. The next moment a challenge comes to that knowledge. If our sense of mastery is not deeply rooted, we may feel doubt about our mastery of our profession. Big changes may come to that profession or career. Our sense of mastery can be totally shaken. For concepts and beliefs are not necessarily connected to our ground of being. For instance beliefs that we must be better than others to be successful in our professions may contradict our essence. Children experience big changes as they grow and as their bodies develop. These challenge their sense of personal identity. Their sense of mastery of the world through their physical body is constantly questioned and shaken. For adults our sense of mastery changes profoundly between the time we are 20 and the time we are 50 or 100.

If the the beliefs and concepts that allow mastery of some ability are interwoven with fears, uncertainties, and apprehensions we will live a life out of balance. If our uncertainties and fears overwhelm any sense of mastery of life, we may become mentally impaired. We also may act out our fears and uncertainties with violence and abuse. We may also confuse the layers of fear with the love which we experience as our basis. From this confusion of fear and love comes all sorts of behavior including all "acting out." Examples are,— sexual acting out in adults or children; defiance and rebellion in children and teenagers; addictions to work, or money, or substances.

THOUGHT PATTERNS
INTERACT AS CHILDREN GROW

The belief in the right to be here in this life does not seem to be a given as children grow older. Their connection to their ground of being may be so seriously damaged that they no longer believe they have a right to be here by virtue of their existence. Many of children's early self-esteem problems develop more fully in their adolescence and early adulthood. Matt, age 27, was struggling to find his way in the adult world. He had, at best, tenuous support from his family, which appeared quite "normal." He learned to distrust what he thought was a conspiring and self-centered world. A world of good and bad, in which the bad was always trying to take things from him or cause him harm. Success was good. Failure was bad. Though a good student, as a young adult Matt's belief in his capacity to succeed was eroding. He had struggled to get a job working for an electrical company, then he was laid off. He went to his father for help but was turned away. At the end of this he found employment but was again laid off. He then became very interested in a young woman who did not return his interest. Feeling rejected he turned to religion. Believing the healing for his failures and fears was in a personal meeting with a television evangelist in another state he stole money and ended up in jail. Matt's sense of his right to be in this life had eroded. He was capable only of basic maintenance. His behavior had become quite erratic. This eventually led to placement in a mental hospital and treatment with therapeutic drugs. It remains for a therapist to reach into this suffering and draw out and strengthen his contact with his ground of being.

Therapy that supports his spiritual quest can help Matt find what he was seeking from the television evangelist. As he gains confidence in his essential worthiness, the sense of loss and failure will be replaced by peace and hope. Had his life included a conscious return to an essence that is positive and life affirming, Matt might have been able to see beyond problems in employment and relationship to eventual success.

The following exercise is helpful in centering ourselves in a quiet place from which the world of suffering and failure can look quite different. A state of mind with little concern about surface thoughts is like a smoothly flowing stream, carrying on its existence in pristine purity.

2. REMEMBERING A QUIET PLACE WITHIN

Eyes closed: This can be done with children of all ages. Be still for a while. Notice the continual flow of thoughts. You are preoccupied with all sorts of problems and issues. You may think of things that have happened in your day, a long time ago or a short time ago. Worries may be constantly on your mind. Breath slowly. Be aware that you are breathing. For a few moments try to go beyond your thoughts. Go deeper within yourself. Try to find a quiet place. Find that place and remember what it feels like. (During your days activities whenever you have a moment, take a few breaths and remember that quiet place.) As you continue you may find that you remember many times when that quiet place was at the center of a moment in you life. Perhaps when you were a child. Perhaps recently. Keep a mental journal of this quiet place. It is always there. Just remembering it will strengthen it. You will find that, as your remembrance is strengthened, your quiet place will be strengthened, too, and so will you. Anxious and fearful thoughts may come to the surface of your mind. Simply let them pass. Don't fight. Let them go. Then return to the quiet. You will begin to notice that these thoughts over time will loose their power to distract you. And in time you will find that the anxiety and fear connected with the thoughts is diminishing.

LAYERS OF CONSCIOUSNESS AND CHILDREN

To see how the layers of consciousness interact, look at a small child who knows he is alive and good and worthy by nature. However, he is also learning to perceive that he is physically small. Out of his sense of worthiness he knows he will be cared for and valued. If one day his trust is violated, and he experiences peril or even violation, and the experience is traumatic enough, it will be retained deep in his mind and body long after he has forgotten it in the shifting pattern of his daily life. But still it is there. It lies like a shadow over his belief in his value and goodness. Perhaps he has come to believe there was something about him that caused this traumatic event to happen — that he is responsible in some way that he can't understand. Another situation arises that may have qualities like the traumatic one, and he may feel an uneasiness and fear that he cannot quite understand. The earlier event is suppressed and seems forgotten. He acts on this uneasiness. Perhaps he feels he wants that experience to go away, so he runs away or lashes out at the person whom he feels is responsible for this reminder. Perhaps he throws a tantrum damaging himself, his playthings, and others. It is possible that each time he is reminded of that earlier experience he will react, and the pattern of reactions will build on one another forming a pattern throughout his life. If the pattern becomes powerful enough, it will be reenacted with the faintest hint of the early experience. If powerful enough it will totally rule his life from a depth that he may not recognize.

DEFENSES TO PROTECT AGAINST REMEMBERING

Adults often react to such scenarios by building up all sorts of defenses against a capricious and cruel world. Adults who have patterns coming from traumas in childhood often train their own children to believe that the world is cruel, capricious, and given to doing harm in unexpected and uncontrollable ways. Yet such training reinforces the pattern and causes it to be stuck. Slowly the child may withdraw from the power of the pattern or act out mindlessly against it. And so the pattern and not the person is in control. His ground of being, in which vitality and confidence, rest becomes buried more and more beneath defense and counter defenses. By the time he is an adolescent he may no longer believe that he is valuable or good — sensing in the pattern an out-of-control and hopeless existence. He may see himself as valueless and bad, or a victim of a cruel world. The original traumatic event has won. It has come to totally dominate his self-perception.

DISSOLVING PATTERNS

When Ian was four and a half his brother was getting a lot of attention for doing well in school. His one-year-old sister was very cute. Ian was acting out by breaking his brother's and sister's toys and ignoring them, and hitting and biting. He felt jealous over a loss of attention. But Ian was also a child of great inner vitality who bounced back after a few minutes of pouting or upset. Because the acting out came and went there was a temptation to ignore it. Ian was not verbal enough to tell us about his problems. Yet we could not ignore them or hope he would grow out of them, because he is also forming a pattern for relating to his brother and sister. Associating, deep within his mind, these siblings with his sense of loss and lack of recognition. To support Ian in forming a more healthy pattern of relationships we needed to give him an avenue of recognition and acknowledgement which was his own. As Ian was a very athletic and buoyant child, he was enrolled in gymnastics. There, over time, he was consistently urged to put his energy into the routines of learning by a skilled teacher. The matter-of-fact approach to each child taking his or her turn in the gymnastics routine helped Ian see to be acknowledged in a situation that included other children's performances.

It was important that Ian had support from his family in dealing with change, the demands of the class, and in assisting him in focusing upon this learning process. Perhaps a four-year-old is not quite ready to learn about himself in depth. But if a family acts to support a child's cooperation with the other children and the teacher, it supports his enjoyment of their company and of the development of his skills and intellectual growth. Family support is a firm hand holding Ian's emotional world steady so that he can feel safe when venturing out. Usually, a four-year-old does not question his right to be here. Certainly Ian felt he was wonderful and perfectly at home on the planet when he was doing anything.

TRAUMAS

We adults attempt to do all we can to prevent children from experiencing any traumatic events. Yet often they happen as a result of uncontrollable events or in very ordinary ways. They may not be necessarily severe, but can be cumulative. That is, a child may experience a constant pattern of disappointments, eg. doing poorly at school assignments, not having various needs met. This may lead to a deep inner pattern in which the child is creating layers of perception of some essential inadequacy or lack of value.

This book is not intended to replace the need for therapy whenever the need arises. If a very traumatic event has happened in a child's life, then that child should have access to very good therapy over a period of time sufficient to help the child recover. Teachers and other public employees in some states are charged with the responsibility of reporting suspected abuse and like traumas to the proper agencies.

DAY-BY-DAY PROBLEMS

As an ongoing way of working with daily upsets and traumas, the exercises in this book (or similar self-knowledge exercises) will help children and adults heal by bringing feelings and issues to the surface in safe situations. By becoming aware of ourselves, we become less willing to act out a series of unconscious patterns upon the world around us. When we consciously decide to act positively upon the world, we begin to dissolve patterns at their root. In calm self-observation, we can see how we decide to do what we do, feel, what we feel, and react as we react. By the time they enter school children already have layers of thoughts that have formed patterns unconsciously directing their behavior and interaction with classmates and teachers. The teaching redundancy and repetition that goes on in classrooms is a result of the attempt to teach on top of all of the unsolved issues that clashing behavior patterns create. A teacher cannot become a therapist and look at each of the myriad issues that a child might be struggling with. But a teacher can create a format in which problems and issues are acknowledged and a child learns some tools to solve or grow — so that problems become stepping stones to success and personal strength. Ignoring issues does not make them go away, and children do not grow out of them, as the thinking of the past insists. If children grew out of problems, we wouldn't have drop outs, crime, and addictions which are destroying our schools.

Central to working with the ideas in this book is a willingness to have a world of love and compassion. It doesn't seem likely at the moment. We are not asked to change the world in order to have a world of compassion and love. What we can do is decide that we are going to be involved in creating, in our own lives, a world of compassion and love. If we start this process, step by step, slowly we will change the world we live in. This has been my experience. And with each step and day that I experience myself moving toward greater peace and acceptance of others, I see the possibility of my world becoming more and more that way. Each day I become more hopeful about changing things that caused me despair in the past.

3. OBSERVATION AND AWARENESS OF CHILDREN

Observe children. Spend a few hours/minutes whenever you have a chance simply observing children. Watch the different ages. Notice the vitality of each child. Watch the ebb and flow. Notice when a child becomes the most vibrant and when, the most clouded, etc. Notice the difference between individual children and children of different ages in their capacity to engage with life, to participate, to become involved quickly and completely. Notice how they each deal with problems and with interactions with each other. After a few days of observing children, observe adults. Notice the differences.

TEACHING AND LEARNING SELF-ESTEEM

We can support self-esteem and emotional health to a greater and greater degree as we promote these qualities in ourselves. We cannot teach our children things that we are not willing to learn ourselves. We cannot teach them respect and compassion if we have only limited or conditional respect and compassion for others. If we respect others only if the do what we want them to do, this conditional respect is experienced as a manipulative way of attempting to control people. We can teach respect more powerfully if we are willing to respect people for doing the very best they can given the information they have. I am awed at the commitment that people have to life. I see individuals making their way against terrible odds, and others getting up again when terrible loss has occurred. Our capacity to create a compassionate and loving world comes from the desire to become more compassionate and loving people. In learning this we will be able to teach it to our children and other adults.

In a sense, we don't teach these things at all. The very youngest members of society have little problem with love and respect. They may have a lack of experience that prevents them from understanding when and why adults are in pain either physically or emotionally. But when they sense a problem, they are often quite spontaneous and comforting. Thus while we teach, we are learning at the same time. More precisely, we are recovering or strengthening our understanding of a part of ourselves that we already know exists but may have forgotten.

SELF-ESTEEM AND TEACHING TECHNICAL SKILLS

Many believe we teach self-esteem by teaching people skills. However in a competitive environment skills are all relative and open to judgment and criticism. When we seem unable to learn skills, we tend to judge ourselves as inadequate and unworthy. In the classroom only a certain number of children get A's. The rest are judged as "less than perfect." And my own experience tells me that those A's are not enough to convince students that they are valuable. The satisfaction gained by winning under these conditions is often tainted, emotionally. The disbursement of grades often reflects complex coping arrangements and power strategies. Many times responses to grades and rankings come into conflict with natural processes of individuation and separation from adult control. These can be read either as rebellion or as healthy formation of adult personality.

In teaching a positive sense of self-worth, we must speak to a child's foundation, beyond his ability to do math or spelling. If he understands that his value exists regardless of his skill development, he can then gain the skill as other parts of his development fall in line with that accomplishment. Children are not all prepared to learn at the same rate at the same time in their lives. By standardizing all learning children are treated as if they are all machines with the same mechanisms for understanding. Our strengths are often in our flexibility and resilience, which allow us to go back to subjects and learn them with greater complexity and depth when we are ready, not when the system tells us to learn. Thus we find women returning to school in their late 20's or 30's doing very well in math and other skills that they had failed to master as adolescents. If we encourage a student's capacity for self-love and understanding, his or her personal processes will expand to contain perceived failures and inadequacies within a context of growing development and mastery. Then the hurts, fears and anxieties will be dissolved, healed, and accepted as part of a whole valuable being.

WE ARE LIMITLESS: AN EMPOWERMENT EXPERIENCE THAT CHANGED MY IDEAS ABOUT WHAT I AM CAPABLE OF DOING

I wish to share with you a recent experience that I had in which I was able to understand how powerful our abilities truly are. I saw that nothing we seek to do is impossible. We can be anything we want to be and accomplish nearly anything. What holds us back? All the messages buried in our mind that tell us it isn't possible. For me, those negative messages dropped away when I participated in a fire walk. Our group process focused upon mental preparation for accomplishing the impossible. After a day of preparation, we started the bonfire. Shortly after this, we did a mock fire walk by walking over a red sleeping bag. Outside I could see the actual bed of coals forming as the assistant raked it to a smooth surface. I started to tremble and shake with fear. In the back of my mind I knew I didn't have to walk across the coals if I didn't want to. Yet the very thought of it had me shaking, and this did not subside until we were standing outside in nearly freezing February temperatures in our bare feet. We started singing songs meaningful to us, — songs calling up our inner resources. There was a sense of powerful connection among the whole group: an overall commitment to one another, to the success of each. Within a few minutes a deep calm came over me. I was no longer shaking. When the first person walked across the hot coals I knew I would too. It was only a question of when. When I stepped out to the front of the trench of red coals, I didn't hesitate or feel fear. I knew, not with my intellect but with my whole being, that there was more to me at this moment than my body. I stepped forward onto the red hot coals and walked five or six steps to the end of the trench. My feet were as normal as they had been before I took the first step. The next the morning they still had traces of charcoal on them but not a single blister. I did another fire walk since that first one. Again fear came up but at a different point in the process. Again I walked several times across the fire with not a single burn. For me, the fire walk was an important empowerment event. Others have their own empowerment processes.

When I completed the fire walk my feelings were beyond description. Nearly everything I had learned about the universe had been turned on its head: my beliefs about the nature of physical reality, and about the way the mind functions. A scientist might give a physiological explanation: that I had simply blocked the pain. But how could I have blocked the pain and come through unscathed? Even a second of exposure to hot steam gives me a blister on my finger. I could feel the heat under every step. I didn't run. Other participants walked back and forth leisurely on the coals. It was as clear to me then as it is now that the universe is not what it appears. Even much of what constituted experience, the solidity of the material world and the laws it seems to obey are open to different interpretations. The physical world may not always obey its own laws. Flesh may not always burn in extreme heat. There may be laws that we have not discovered that explain what happened. We may discover principles that radically alter our perception of our physical and mental worlds.

I felt an amazing sense of freedom from what in the past had seemed my personal limitations. If I can do this, then I can do anything. Had I maintained that feeling, I would have experienced no limits in my life. But my whole ground had been layered with fears and anxieties in response to many experiences in life. I had become cautious because I believed in my limitation. As the days passed the memory moved away. But not completely. My fire walk teacher who does these walks many times a year struggles with his own life as well. What I then understood intellectually, and knew to be true for hours after the fire walk, was that there is nothing that binds us, nothing that has to be so. Yet this conclusion must become the bedrock foundation of my being if I am to be truly free and completely masterful at all times. If I can believe this in myself with consistency to the degree that I did during the firewalk then I would have a permanent attitude of joy. For at this degree of purity, freedom and joy are indistinguishable.

There was an element in the fire walk that involved the group belief system as well. When our traditional beliefs about fire fell, every participant was able to drop his or her individual attitudes and limitations. Each benefitted from the other's successful crossing of the coals. I often wonder if we could have been so successful without one another.

EACH DAY CAN BE A WELCOMING TO LIFE

When an adult speaks to the essence of a child, the adult communicates to the part of the mind that has the potential for walking on fire, for accomplishing the miraculous. I believe that our job as adults is to bring that forth in each and every child so that their lives can be miraculous and profound. That is the ultimate goal of working with self esteem-issues.

We all need to be reminded that we are welcomed here on this earth, that we are here to be happy, and to participate fully. That we do not have to prove our right to be here, that we have that right by virtue of our existence. Variations on this exercise inspired by John Bradshaw's work can be utilized for this purpose.(1.) Any other "I'm glad you are you" exercise will work as well. Mr. Rogers has been doing this for years for his neighbors in his neighborhood.

4. WELCOME TO THE WORLD

This exercise can be done with two or more individuals. Focus upon one person at a time. Speak in quiet voices as if speaking to angels. You should feel comfortable and safe. If you wish, use a cuddly toy or blanket. The participants affirm to one person at a time:

I'm glad you are here.
I'm happy you're a boy (girl).
God smiled when you were born.
The universe rejoices that you came.
Without you, the universe would be incomplete.
All nature and being smiles on your birth.
You (name) are valued. There is nothing you need to do to justify your being here.
You (name) have the right to be here.
You are the fulfillment of life's energy and wishes.
You (name) are here to be happy.
All you need do is choose to be happy.
You (name) are love and you are loved.

At first you or participating children may find these exercises silly or uncomfortable. But with continued use the messages will work, past all of the fears and suffering to a deep vitality within.

We have within us the capacity to do and be beyond our imagination. It is possible for adults to assist children in staying in touch with a vision of themselves, a vision that will empower them to a blossoming of their lives in which they reach toward their own inner greatness. Children are often much closer to experiences of limitlessness than are adults. They can also be our teachers in learning about the essence of our power.

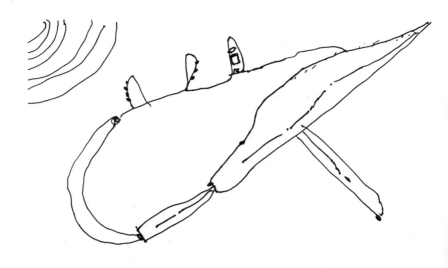

Footnote:

(1.) John Bradshaw, "Home Coming, Reclaiming and Championing Your Inner Child," New York, Bantam Books, 1992, p 96.

2. PRAISE

The answer to every self-esteem issue for ourselves and the children in our lives lies in how we approach one another. If we see ourselves as having the answers for others lives we will believe that everyone needs correction. We will demand perfection of a type determined by outside models. We will be critical and we will punish when those we try to instruct or control fail. We will intrude deeply within another's self-perception, suggesting that it does not measure up, does not fit some ultimate criteria. While the foundation of self-worth remains beyond our capacity to damage, the other person's self-perception will, in time, become layered over with messages which conflict with one another. A confusion of don'ts. In a frantic effort to respond to an onslaught of demands, this individual may cease to be able to find her/his way to that quiet place within.

To make a pot, a potter begins by throwing a piece of clay down onto a wheel. She then starts the wheel spinning at a fairly high rate of speed. Then she puts fingers from one hand down into the clay forming an indentation while she holds the other hand outside to support the clay. As the pot forms she slowly lifts the clay upward from within and presses back inward from the outside. If the pressure and the flow upward are fairly equal, a symmetrical vessel will rise to whatever height or size the amount of clay will allow. A potter who is skilled at this support system can create elaborate forms.

When we deal with other humans it is a good idea to keep this model in mind. The pot cannot be made without support from the outside. The outside hand holds the clay against the pressure of the inside hand. If the pressure is uneven the pot immediately becomes lopsided and falls apart. If we direct a child in very specific ways, we may be touching into the depths of his consciousness. We need to have a supportive hand which constantly reminds him that he is living in a compassionate and loving world, so that we are not teaching him to distrust himself or question his right to be.

SOCIETAL SHOULD'S

As we learn to approach other humans with reverence, we will come to revere ourselves and restore our own capacity to see past our blocks. We can learn a different way of seeing that pays less and less attention to the confusion of images outside of ourselves. When we try to force societal shoulds and ideals of appearance and achievement upon our own self-image, we distort our sense of ourselves. The outside hand has become too heavy. Children want to please, and they turn to adults to guide them in learning how to be part of the world. If the guidance is done with tenderness, the child can keep his integrity, and self-love. If a child is constantly expected to fit a mold he may see himself as an error. He will feel at odds with himself. He will act out of the conflict between his feelings of what is right for him and the behaviors that others expect of him.

When I say that societal shoulds have a coercive and distorting effect on people, many will respond that this means not teaching "values." Yet if values were not our natural inheritance, we would all be incapable of doing or being good. Values are ours by birth. We are loving and compassionate. Loving and compassionate people have positive, or good values. It is difficult to accept that as much as we train children in positive values, we, of the adult world, also train them in negative values.

Children and adults are, in essence, equals, just as the sexes and various races are equal. As we help children and others to interact with an often frightening, complex and overwhelming world, we must fill each step of guidance with support, with positive feed back that builds one step at a time.

Praising others is often difficult for people who are raised in dour household environments, where very little praise was given. If they experience constant demands and relentless criticism, they are not in the habit of receiving positive regard. After having consciously practiced giving praise, I have come to believe that compliments do not perpetuate vanity. In the past I, saw praise as a way of manipulating another for ulterior purposes or to show off, making a spectacle of oneself. Because I must deal with these anti-praise beliefs, I often do a very clumsy job at praising others. I tend to want to fall back on a lifetime of habit of criticism and complaint.

Praise given in order to elicit a specific response, or to get something from another person is limited in value and will do very little to support another's self-esteem. This behavior is really not praise but flattery; in which each person puts a price upon the outcome and often both are disappointed. Flattery comes from the belief that people will not do things out of their own desire to do good. It reinforces beliefs that humans are innately willful and disobedient. If we believe that we must force people to be good, we perpetuate this belief by using flattery and manipulation. As an adult, because I did not trust praise, I attempted to manipulate people to meet my needs. However, as time went on, I found that this approach did not work. My needs were not being met, and manipulation was not working. I was forced to learn other ways of coping, new approaches.

I learned that gratitude facilitates changing from criticism to praise. I learned to consciously appreciate what I had previously taken for granted — to appreciate the support of others, even if it doesn't come in the form that I want. Praise, in its most powerful form, is an acknowledgement of the good in the world, a way of saying thanks. Praise, like most practices in this book, is a process. The more we approach pure appreciation, the more powerful will our acts of praise become — when our heartfelt praise helps a child or adult to feel that his or her contribution is valuable. Praise others because they are wonderful by nature. Their lives are a gift to us.

5. GRATITUDE

Observation exercise: Notice all of the events, feelings, aspects of your life for which you could or do feel grateful. Look around you. Take it all in. Allow yourself to experience the fullness of it all, the fullness of life. See the people in your life. See the abundance. See the beauty. Smell it, hear it. Let it fill your body and mind. Let it be there within you.

Each of us needs to develop habits that counter any deeply etched personal patterns of negative feedback to support the changes that we want. Develop ways that are caring and compassionate rather than destructive and divisive. If I want a child or an adult to stop hitting or being abusive, I can praise her when she is kind. I can say how much I appreciate that kind of behavior, how glad I feel about what she is doing, and what a joy it is to be around a loving and sensitive person. In the past I might have criticized that person for how she behaved when the behavior was not what I wanted. Now I find myself resisting the impulse to tell her she is bad or disappointing. I save my complaints for my diary saying only the loving things. I am not always successful at this and at times I still moan and groan and carry on.

It is important to say "no" when you are being violated. It is important to assert your own needs. We don't praise in situations in which behavior is ambivalent or questionable. I wouldn't acknowledge a person who was being rude or destructive. I would look for the time when he remained calm in an upsetting situation and say, "I notice that you didn't go along with the feeling that you wanted to hit. I think that is great. It really shows how much you care about yourself and others."

Take a chance and say something positive. You may feel awkward and embarrassed at first, but go ahead. As you practice this, you'll see changes you attempted to create via your complaints come via your praise. In praising our own children we are countering, perhaps, generations of stoicism and hypercritical behavior. We all make mistakes. Children make mistakes. We know that people make mistakes and difficult things happen, sometimes very painful things happen; however, every person is worthy and has the right to be here. We praise and celebrate another human's wonderfulness.

PRAISE AND ACHIEVEMENTS

Praise that focuses on the accomplishments of a person is of limited value because it confuses the person with the skill. He will become a human "doing" rather than a human "being." He may try to crank out all sorts of awards, projects, or skills in order to earn the positive feedback. Meanwhile, the being within becomes more and more confused about what is his real worth. He will think that he must do these things in order to justify being on this planet. It is fine to praise accomplishments as long as we do not forget to value the person, not what he can do for us.

I have learned to create daily practices of giving praise. The following exercise and suggestions will help you create daily practices of your own:

6. PRAISE

Interactive exercise: never miss an opportunity to praise. Praise when you would rather have complained. Praise whenever you remember to and when you forget. Think of 100 positive things about another when you think of something negative. Make a list of why you love the people in your life. Put the list on your mirror, on the refrigerator, in the car, in your wallet or purse. Read it often. Write love notes to others. Put notes everywhere to remind yourself to say something positive to your children. Begin to praise everyone you interact with. Don't worry about making a mess of it. With practice you will get better and better. Notice your feelings and difficulties around praising others. It's a great self-discovery device. Notice how you feel when others praise you.

Just thinking positive things is a very powerful process. It weeds out the unhappy, negative and distrustful thought patterns at the surface of the mind. As we say positive things, we trigger all sorts of emotions and memories within the mind. As we find the means to praise, we are repatterning our thoughts. Often we can do so while the world about us continues in old practices and behaviors. Children and adults will forgive you if your positive regard is not conveyed with great skill. As you start praising you will find those you praise drawn closer to you. You may even find this frightening. This closeness is what we all yearn for. It is why we came to this life. Allowing ourselves to be praised becomes easier when we practice praise. Practice continuously and you will begin to experience praise as a flow of joy.

RESISTING PRAISE

I noticed that a second grader who was doing very well in school was very upset by my praise. I was very careful to tell him that I knew that he was great. His accomplishments were a reflections of a terrific boy. Yet, he didn't want anyone to know what he had done. I realized that his self-criticism had become so persistent, he did not trust any praise or positive regard from others.

7. LET THE GOOD IN

(For eyes closed guided images, you can use music to create a relaxed state.) Remember something that you did that was wonderful. See the time that it happened. What temperature was it? What did it smell like? Who was with you? What were you wearing? How did you feel when this wonderful thing happened? Now feel what a wonderful person you are to have done such a thing. Now tell yourself in your own mind: "I am wonderful because it is my nature to be wonderful. I am beautiful like a sunset. I am capable like the wind that blows away the haze. I am loving and refreshing like the rain that helps plants to grow. I am good like all of life is good." Now think of something that another person you know has done that was good. See that time. What was it like? What did it feel like? How did that person look, smell and talk? Stand in front of that person and in your mind tell him or her. "You are wonderful like the world. (You can make up these parts as it suits you.) It is in your nature to do good because you are a loving and capable person. You are like the energy in a plant that pushes up through rocks as it buds in the spring." Now see how you feel about what you did. When you are through with this image share your feelings with the other adults and/or children.

We may feel conned or that the praise-giver wants something from us. We think if we get caught up by praise that we might be disappointed when praise is withdrawn. In order to strengthen our ability to communicate positively with others, we need to be able to accept the praise that others give. Many of us who have come from criticism-oriented and negative-feedback backgrounds may have a great deal of difficulty letting in praise. We may have numbed ourselves so that we don't feel it, or acknowledge that we need and appreciate positive support. We may deflect praise with some self-deprecating statement like, "It was really nothing." Or we may become very distrustful of praise-givers. It seems too embarrassing. Others may notice the praise and become jealous. They may say something cruel like, "He thinks he's so hot!" It is important that we understand that praise or positive regard are totally natural ways of interacting with others — just as natural as breathing. We breath in the praise of others and breath out our praise for others.

Guided images are helpful in going through experiences in the past and working through our conflicting emotions. This is a private process that helps a person notice and acknowledge embarrassment, resistance and anger that comes up when she is praising or being praised.

When infants learn to walk and talk, they practice continuously and are encouraged. They learn in the most natural way. Their desire to learn is powerful. Watch babies. They fall down and get up. They take the next step without concern for success. We all have equally powerful desires to learn everything possible in this lifetime. The facilitator for this learning is positive feedback. If the level and amount of positive feedback is doubled or even tripled the results are phenomenal. This is the most efficient way to motivate others. With practice, as we become self-aware, we will learn to make every communication of positive regard heartfelt and sincere.

8. FEELINGS ABOUT PRAISE

Examine your feelings as you praise, and determine what keeps you from praising others. Learn to put those feelings behind you; they are too costly to your own happiness and that of others in your life. Forgive the hurts and disappointments of your past. As you forgive, those around you will also be able to let go of the damage in the past.

With time, we can all learn to give positive feedback from the deepest places within us. We must begin now and continue day by day.

3. EXERCISES

Practice is the heart and soul of this approach to building self-esteem. Just as we have healthy bodies when we eat right, exercise, and live in healthful ways, we learn to strengthen our self-esteem by nurturing our mental health. As adults, we can clearly see our progress as the years and months go by. However, children have a limited sense of personal history. Children are not as clearly able to control their lives. Nor do they have the perspective to see the relationship between their self-perception and the way they interact with the world. Adults can provide ongoing nurturing for positive self-worth, and a structure in which a child can view his progress.

This book's exercises are divided into three categories: 1. exercises for quieting the mind and introspection; 2. exercises in which we observe ourselves and the world around us; 3. exercises in which we use what we've learned from within and from observation to interact with the world.

EYES-CLOSED EXERCISES

We all day dream. Some of the eyes-closed exercises are consciously created day dreams. We can see ourselves at other times in our lives. We can see problems we have faced in the past. And we can see ourselves as happy and fulfilled. When we realize that it is OK just to be ourselves and to have the feelings and thoughts that we have, we relax. When we relax we are less stressed, and this is good for the body and as a preparation for acting in life. A relaxed state helps us find answers even in tense circumstances.

With inner work, we quiet the mind and use images to notice feelings within. A quiet mind allows us to become aware of the subtlety of feelings and experiences. When we are agitated or our thoughts are obsessive, information from our bodies and our feelings must reach crises level before we pay attention. Our lives then are spent attempting to deal with these crisis. A quiet mind allows us to notice problems and issues early and facilitates solving them. A quiet and peaceful mind is prepared for the next moment whether it brings a math exam, or a traumatic incident.

In eyes-closed exercises we recall experiences from the past, and we gain insights about why we act in certain ways. We learn how our behaviors are connected to certain experiences and feelings. I used this process recently to deal with my eating habits. I paid attention to feelings that would lead me to want to eat. I wanted to eat every time I felt uncomfortable or unhappy. One day I decided to visualize myself being comforted without eating. To this day, I have been able to drop my unnecessary eating. I made a conscious choice to become aware of feelings which lie behind unconscious behavior. Then I stopped the behavior. We need not lead unconscious lives in which we have no idea why we do what we do.

OBSERVATION EXERCISES

In the second group of exercises we practice observation, which is the backbone of any scientific work. Each and every step of a theory is tested and demonstrated to be either valid or invalid. We constantly test who we are by observing ourselves. In these exercises, we can learn to continue the practice of observation as a link between introspective and interactive exercises.

In order to know who we are and how we behave, think or interact, it is important that we learn to observe ourselves and others as thoroughly and with as much detachment as possible. (In science detachment might be considered objectivity.) Observation exercises can help to develop this detachment. We observe regularly, and we learn to watch ourselves. If we do not judge, impinge upon, or affect what is happening, we may learn to see our experiences from a different perspective. Perhaps we can see another's perspective. As we observe our destructive attitudes and behaviors, we find we have less compulsion to act in ways harmful to ourselves and others. For instance if I notice that I have prejudice toward East Indian people but I also notice that they have their own perspective, my observations may help me let go of my racism. This difficult process doesn't demand that we decide immediately whether something is bad or good. Detachment is developed when we desire to be objective and not when when inject all of our fears, and insecurities. When we detach we are free to act with compassion and caring.

When I interact with adolescents, my past experience and training has taught me to compulsively stop them from behaving badly or acting out just as I was stopped when I was an adolescent. If I stop them I reinforce the negative behavior by labeling it bad, something to be stopped. Instead I struggle against all of my inner programming to stop disruptive adolescent behavior in order to see them just as they are, and all of the problems that each of us has. First I must observe myself, and become responsible for my part in the relationship. Detachment allows me to notice unresolved feelings from my adolescence, and then become calm. Adolescent reaction to my inner conflict is replaced by a response to my calmness. The disruptive behavior often subsides.

INTERACTIVE EXERCISES

The third exercise group involves exchanges between ourselves and others. This group includes listening, talking, drama, touching, goal processes,and journal work. In interactive exercises, we can practice our strengthened sense of self-esteem in a setting that protects its new-born vulnerability and helps prepare us for less supportive realities of society. When we try our listening and talking skills in a nurturing environment, though we might be beginners, we won't fear ridicule or criticism.

USING THE DIFFERENT TYPES
OF EXERCISES TOGETHER

The ideal is to combine these processes regularly. If we can practice quieting the mind, observation from a more detached or compassionate perspective, and practice this compassion through interactive processes, we will be adding a new pattern of balance to our lives. We can learn to live in a connected process of interactions. Think of it as breathing in and breathing out. Breath in and feel how you want to be and breath out and try it out. When we feel the flow between inner exploration and outward action, we have a deep sense of fulfillment and contentment, and mastery of life. Each of us may need a specific mixture of these processes, more of one and less of another. But it is important that we are involved in all. Being conscious of this tripod helps us to make sure that all of our needs are met.

9. INTEGRATION EXERCISE
SIMPLIFIED FOR YOUNG CHILDREN

First close your eyes. Notice your thoughts. Be aware of what you are feeling. Be aware of what is going on inside of your body. Now open your eyes. See what is happening outside of you. What is going on in the world? What does it all look, smell, and feel like? What kind of world is it that you live in? Notice the people and all the things that are important and unimportant to you. Now talk to someone about what you see. Notice how that person talks to you. Notice how you feel when that person talks to you. In your daily life notice what you see inside of yourself and what you see when you are observing the world.

Now close your eyes again and see what you notice there. How do you feel about this process? What did you like about it? What didn't you like about it? Now tell yourself that it was OK to like some parts and dislike others. It was just like life with all of its parts. Now tell yourself that you are fine. That you are perfect just as you are doing life the best you can. Be happy.

By doing a similar mixture of exercises, I have learned to interact with the world — to bring what I have learned about my essential self-worth with me. So, when things do not go smoothly, I am not so troubled by it. I don't take it so seriously or personally. Because I know that I am OK and that perhaps this roughness is a sign that I am changing and growing. In my process I notice I am reacting to the possibility of things going smoothly. I notice I had the same sort of reaction when I first learned to quiet my own mind. I remember I hated it in some ways. Thought it was mind control. I was also surprise by how good it felt and wanted more of that feeling. I notice that I can interact fully and freely with my work and other activities, knowing I have a place to refuel, a place of quiet to feel truly good about myself and not be subject to judgments and opinions. I know it is a process: as I learn to master myself, I will have greater mastery of the world.

Children are often treated as receptacles for information, emotions and effects from the adult world. They too need to find their own balance, one in which they can integrate their experiences while interacting with the world. If in doing so they feel understood and valued, and in turn value and understand the world, they will feel at harmony with themselves and life.

In Appendix A I have adapted the exercises for children between kindergarten and the sixth grade. Exceptions are generally noted in the exercises. Exercises involving touching or discussions of sex need to be conducted by adults who have extensive understanding of their own feelings about physical and sexual boundaries.

10. CONSCIOUS BREATHING

Close your eyes and pay attention to natural, continuous breath coming through your nostrils. Breath going in. Breath coming out. Breath going through the right nostril, or the left, or both nostrils. When a thought begins, gently replace it with breath. Do not fight the thoughts but return again to breath. If it is hard to keep your attention on the breath, just breathe a bit harder for a while. In doing this with children or other adults, rhythmically tell them quietly to "Breath in. Breath out. Experience the breath coming in and going out." In time they can learn to notice the process of thoughts coming and going, as well.

BREATHE AND QUIET THE MIND

The Conscious Breathing exercise is a simple example of how one exercise can work toward changing long-term patterns of thinking and stress on the body.

When a child learns to breath consciously five minutes each day at school or home, it gradually becomes part of daily life. Five minutes of consciously breathing in and out allows the body and mind to rest. This exercise creates alpha wave patterns in the brain, which current medical research show strengthen the immune system and help keep the body healthy. With practice the child's mind relaxes and produces alpha wave patterns more quickly.

In addition, repetition of the exercise brings peace and a sense of well being that increases confidence in interacting with other children and in completing school work. The child will learn how to consciously cause this change in her life at any time or place she chooses. A person can call upon this technique as a response to upsetting or frightening experiences, or for times when she felt she needed to be at peace and care for her mental and physical health. She would appreciate the need for balance in dealing with her own health, with interactions with other people, and while working.

Breathing consciously can help to detach us from emotions, events, and problems in our lives. Greater detachment brings a greater sense of control and mastery over our bodies and lives. It also brings greater compassion, because, when we can stand back a bit from our own troubles, we are able to see things from a new perspective that may include someone else's point of view. Conscious Breathing can break the cycle of fixating and obsessing upon personal problems or bodily ills. Obsessions stress us, quiet heals us.

I have used breathing when working with children in a classroom. If a child is having a hard time with the curriculum, I sit with the student and we breathe together. After a short while she relaxes and then her frustrations or sense of hopelessness lessens. This allows her to return to the task with new focus. When a child realizes she can stop and relax, she feels in control. Being fresh, alert, and aware again also allows her to call upon all of her intelligence and override panic or forced attention that comes when she feels unable to do the work.

Ultimately a child can see her success as part of an ongoing process in which this period of quiet forms a nurturing base. Obstacles and apparent failures slowly lose their capacity to sway the child's attention and goals, because she is able to stand aside and observe her life from the perspective that quietness gives. Success now comes in its own time. She knows that she is ultimately able to deal with or overcome the obstacles to that success. "I am a success at life already," she says. "I can move from this success to other ways of dealing with life in a natural manner."

OBJECTIONS TO BREATHING

It is hard to believe that people feel threatened by the act of breathing. But many adults are skeptical of anything different. The weight of recent scientific research on breathing or quieting the mind is beginning to fall solidly behind any practice that helps children and adults maintain a sense of well-being and calm while coping with stress-filled lives. Breathing is so ordinary as to be beyond any attempts to interpret it as being dangerous. Our ability to control where our attention goes by focusing on our breath is strengthened each time we do this exercise. As we see day by day that we can control our mind and our thoughts, we see that we are not controlled by them. Conscious Breathing becomes the foot of a compass that brings us back to a sense of wholeness and well-being.

INNER OBJECTIONS TO SELF-ESTEEM

A conscious breathing exercise, like many of the exercises in this book, will probably proceed in stages. Perhaps there will be enthusiasm at first because it is so simple. Perhaps participants will feel enthusiastic because it brings achievable results. (The exercises are entirely free with the exception of the time involved.) As we begin to have some success, old patterns of mind and behavior will resist change. We may want to stop doing the exercises. Success in strengthening self-esteem meets many obstacles which confront any effort toward success in life. In order to nurture a positive self-image, we need to learn to ignore all objections that suggest all was better before we started these silly, unusual, or controversial exercises. Success in self-esteem means digging in for a long term commitment to ourselves.

UNLEARNING

The learning processes for self-esteem are often unlearning processes. We come to recognize beyond the plethora of information that we get from the world our goodness and internal beauty cannot be diminished. We often feel inadequate in the face of all the messages we get from outside about how to live our lives, how much money to have, what we should know and look like. No one can live up to the expectations of others. Furthermore, it is often very difficult to live up to our expectations for ourselves, which have been inflated by the messages that constantly raise the stakes on possessions and success.

Our unlearning is accomplished by involving all of our senses and emotions as well as our mind. In that regard it is very different from academic learning, which requires the intellect and a surface level of mental activity. In order to read a book or solve a math equation, we rarely call upon deeper mental levels, for instant the mind-body mental connection, the unconscious and so forth. Yet our most powerful learning involves all of our being, our emotions, our bodies as well as our intellect. Great, innovative, intellectual breakthroughs bring all of our being together to reach a point beyond which we only imagined. When we each reach into our sources of personal greatness, we summon them forth with all that is in us. Just as an Olympic gold medalist moves past fear and gives every ounce of his or her being for the ultimate performance.

You may tell yourself "I have a positive self-image," over and over again for weeks and months. But if you don't believe deep within your whole being, your progress toward believing it will be very slow. When you can completely open our feelings, your heart, your deepest levels of your mind, and your experiences to accept that you are very worthy, then you will act and think as a person who has a powerful positive view of herself. With a positive expectation of life, we come to have a mastery of life. Our feelings, mind and experiences accept what is nurturing of that self-image and this in turn strengthens the positive self-esteem even further. This is a process of unlearning or letting go of deep thoughts of unworthiness and replacing them with powerful reconnections with our innate value.

MULTILEVEL LEARNING

If children or adults have very low or negative self-esteem, initially, they may want to reject each effort to nurture a positive self-image. They may not trust the support they are receiving. And they may find ways of perceiving positive acts and support as negative. The exercises will help these adults and children get past the mind's need to reject something so different from its apparent surface system of thought. They must unlearn a poor self-image. Exercises that speak to emotions, the body and the deeper levels of consciousness and intellect reach that part of the mind that knows it's OK. This will resonate with the ground of being and facilitate accepting the support. In time this interaction with nurturing and positive support will build strong links with mental structure so that objections and resistance do not interfere.

Logical explanations and intellectual solutions to problems surrounding self-esteem are not always the answer. We cannot argue a child into feeling good about himself no matter how solid our logic. In fact, when arguing, we interact with that part of the child that automatically rejects that support. This is merely overcoming a child's resistance to feeling good about himself by attempting to force information upon him. Many teachers and parents find this reaction particularly true for adolescents who have built defenses to keep adults out. Yet even adolescents can be reached by constant and patient application of self-esteem nurturing processes.

Kindergarten teachers are coming to understand that if they involve all of the senses and emotions in learning, the learning takes place more quickly. This is why children learn to walk and talk so quickly and directly. In involving all of the child in the process of strengthening self-esteem, the learning (or unlearning of dysfunctional beliefs) is more powerfully direct and effective. Without involving feelings and even the body senses and only appealing to the intellect, the process of empowering children's self-esteem will be far longer and more laborious. As an ongoing interaction it needs to go beyond surface jargon and terms to be memorized and recited. Jargon and memorized words can be forgotten; whereas, once children test out the value of their true strengths in a supportive setting, they will be inclined to maintain them. That is, kids like to feel good about themselves and, if given the chance, will like the process. When they are given one course every now and then, they don't learn to transfer that self-perception to every area of their lives. It is in its transfer to all of life where the capacity of positive self-esteem to totally transform schools, families, children and ultimately the whole planet resides.

GROUND RULES

It is very important that certain ground rules are set in order to make your atmosphere for the exercises as safe as possible for all participants. At the top of any list of ground rules would be: 1. No put downs, personal attacks, or criticism. 2. Confidentiality. That is, no reporting on what happens within the process to people not involved. At first people are very tender when revealing even a little bit of themselves. Protect this tenderness as you would the new growth of a plant in the garden. 3. Each participant is to take responsibility for his/her own behavior and experiences, and his/her responses to the behavior and communication of others. This means not attaching blame to anyone for the bad feelings that you have when you get angry about something. 4. Be aware. Be aware of yourself and your responses. Being aware helps us to keep inventories of patterns of mental response and behavior. If I become aware that I always get hungry when someone is angry with me, I can learn to stop using food to deal with that feeling. And perhaps I can take a chance and talk about how anxious I feel when someone is angry.

It may take a while for these simple guidelines to be observed as rigorously as is necessary to allow the process to function fully. Furthermore, teachers or parents may consider, at some point, acting on information that surfaces when working with children, e.g. information about abuse. It is important for teachers to communicate that there are conditions under which confidentiality may be broken so that children can decide what it is that they wish to communicate. In this way the integrity of the children and of the process is not violated. If we don't give a child a chance to decide when and how they will reveal themselves, then we have undermined this process. We may believe that children are not mature enough to decide when or where to tell things. Yet, when we make a decision to control their thinking and feeling, we prevent them from feeling in control of their thoughts and feelings. A child won't tell us of his sadness if he feels it might endanger his whole universe, his security, and the source of what he sees as love. If he is allowed to tell of his sadness, he can tell us from his sense of his own strength. Self-esteem processes are not fact-finding ventures for child protective agencies. They are intended as ongoing tools that help children long after child protective actions have occurred. Also teachers can come to respect the process children go through so that they are prepared to report and deal with the information.

NO PUT DOWNS

In working with children from the second grade upward I have found that it may take many sessions before rule #1 (safety) is observed. By the second grade, criticism, put downs, and verbal attacks are so common that it may take many sessions to deal with the issue of these very painful behaviors. (Incidentally, within a multilevel use of processes, children can begin to see the relationship between attacks and how they feel about themselves not simply when they are being attacked but also when they are attacking.)

VULNERABLE INFORMATION

It is better that children be allowed and perhaps even encouraged not to communicate personal or vulnerable material early in processes. You may want to limit debriefing communications to indirect approaches such as writing in journals, drawings or games. Or encourage children to put insights into plays, rather than talking about them with other children. Children by nature of their personality development have yet to learn their own boundaries. The process of learning boundaries is an ongoing one for children at each age. So the rule of non-disclosure may also be treated as a process. That is, you can talk about telling on people and how that feels, and why we don't do it unless absolutely necessary. As children, adolescents, and adults learn to work with the processes they will begin to see how to communicate safely. If they do this too quickly, the process may become unsafe early on, and you will have to regain trust.

However, I do not suggest to simply return to "show and tell." Though "show and tell" personalizes a child's experience, it adds very little to self-understanding or the classmates' understanding. I observed a third grade class where the teacher instructed the children to write a short essay about the good qualities of the "student of the week." The teacher broadened the children's vocabulary while adding to each child's self-esteem. While sharing allows children to answer in "I feel..." statements. For example if asked what his favorite thing at home is, the child can answer, "I like my cat because she feels soft and warm. I feel happy when I see her purring." This supports positive experiences and the process of communicating about all experiences, rather than simply an enumeration of possessions. Ownership as discussed in a "show and tell" setting is far less satisfying and self-worth building than talking about who we really are and how we feel. Unfortunately "show and tell" continues throughout High School paraded in cars, clothes, and status symbols that create very strong group identification based on possessions rather than personal attributes.

LOGISTICS

Parents and teachers who utilize these exercises can make all sorts of guidelines about the level of activity; about how long the processes should take; about location; and about behavior during the exercises. These parameters can vary and support the "Safe Space" quality. Guidelines may vary depending upon the age group.

In special education classes I have seen controlled communication processes like the Insight Exercise(page 90) used with adolescents who have a history of acting out and may be under court supervision. In these classes, specific types of communications are allowed. The participants communicate complaints only if they are within the context of an "I feel" statement, e.g., "When you did this (act/behavior) I felt — and so I object to it." Within this context they also were to make statements in support of one another, as well as constructive proposals for changes. In a sense, a script was written by the teachers in charge in order to have a constructive interaction and to avoid the high level of acting out (violence, crime, sexualizing) that was already normal for these students.

AGES AND LEVELS

Unless otherwise specified, the exercises in this book are for all ages and levels of understanding. Guidelines and settings may be varied in order to adapt the exercises to each age and group.

OTHER EXERCISES

There are many nurturing activities not listed in the contents of this book that adults can do with each other and with children. Here is a partial list of alternative activities: planting a garden; writing and performing music together that expresses personally meaningful communication; creating personally meaningful art together such as murals or quilts; cooking meals and foods that nurture and deepen experiences of togetherness.

11. THE EXERCISE EXERCISE

Make up a fun, self-exploration exercise. Make up an exercise for things you find difficult. Make up an exercise for learning new ways to play games with others. Make up an exercise for new ways that you can tell others about yourself, and they can tell you about themselves. Make up an exercise for fun ways to do work. Make up an exercise everytime there is something very hard or painful in your life, an exercise that will help you find a way to work with that difficulty and that pain. Create your own exercise to support self-esteem. Let children create their own self-esteem exercises.

4. SILENCE AND NONVERBAL COMMUNICATION

The very basis for our ground of being lies in silence. Silence perhaps as deep and ancient as the silence of the universe. We are born out of the silence of our mother's inner world. Nearly half of our first days and months are the quiet world of dreams and sleep. Only slowly do we come to the energy of the world beyond us.

We treasure stillness, quiet, and peace. Think of the moments in your life when you felt the most complete, the most loved, the most at home. As you remember those times you will begin to notice that there was a quality of inner peace about them. To maintain this inner peace at all times would give us the capacity to go through the many changes of life without panic, stress, or suffering. This is good for our health and well-being as well as for the people around us.

All forms of conscious inner quiet ground us. In this chapter I will include many exercises in becoming quiet. They will help you to relax, release anxiety, and live a balanced life. In this quiet lies a basis of self-esteem so powerful that should you live completely out of it, you can make contributions to life far beyond your imaginings. You may choose among these exercises or find other forms to suit you. However, I would urge you to find a way to have silence for a few minutes each day. Preferably morning and night. I urge teachers to include minutes of quiet breathing or guided imagery, devoid of "work," in their classroom schedule. This is a spiritual practice in the deepest sense but need have no connection with any known religion. At its core the experience of peace tells us that we are fine just the way we are.

If you practice the Awareness Exercise for a few minutes on a daily basis, you will begin to understand how your intellect and your other forms of consciousness interact. You will also begin to see that you have the capacity to control your conscious thoughts. This will also help you to more easily reach into deeper parts of the mind.

12. AWARENESS

Go to a quiet place. Try sitting indoors. Alternate this with sitting in nature. Be consciously aware of everything. Be consciously aware of your breathing. Be aware of your emotions and feelings. Be aware of your body. Be aware of sounds around you. Be aware of physical movement. Be aware of smells. Be aware of the visual world. Notice how, when you begin to allow thoughts about concerns other than what is going on in this silence to dominate your awareness, you begin to loose your sensitivity to the subtlety of what you are experiencing. Be aware of how your patterns of thought try to pull you away. Be aware of the patterned nature of your thoughts. Be aware of the thoughts about simply being there. Notice how your awareness changes and deepens.

SELF-DISCIPLINE

Gaining the discipline to spend time quietly is often difficult for us. Surface patterns of the mind do not want to be controlled. Obsessive mental patterns tend to be out of control. When you start practicing quiet, you may find many reasons not to do it. You may believe that it is mind-washing or some other bad procedure. But the mind longs for this quiet. Recognize this longing as an experience of relief at being silent at last. This part of the mind welcomes the quiet as does the parched earth when rain finally comes. Yet gaining peace is as simple as the above exercise and has no negative ulterior motive. Retreats and groups can also offer support for practicing quiet, if we need it.

Our frantic, crowded, action-filled society has deep prejudices against this sort of activity. That is why it is so needed, particularly, by children. In childhood we were trained to grow away from this quietness. Too few in the adult world acknowledge or understand it's importance. Often being quiet is considered a sign of laziness, stupidity, or lack of initiative. Children grow away from their natural relationship to silence, they feel the loss acutely. They come to fill this sense of loss with constant activity. In quiet, they become aware that all they really need to do on this planet is be. Out of this realization comes incredible freedom, and, ironically, permission to do wonderful things, to participate in ways beyond the limits that compulsive action imposes. I have worked with young children who are so anxious to please, to do thing right, that they cannot concentrate on tasks.

You can guide children and other adults in Awareness or Conscious Breathing Exercises (see page 30). They are good exercise to do in the early morning. Practicing quiet assists us in maintaining a central core of peace, which is natural for us. This core allows you to be poised and alert at all times, to be ready and to be relaxed at the same time. This is a quality of strength. It means that stress will not reach into this place and upset your essential quietness, and your body will be protected from stresses contributing to illness, especially heart disease and cancer.

THINKING

Thoughts cannot harm society. However, verbal statements or actions do. Thoughts, when held within, when suppressed and pushed down inside the subconscious mind, do not dissipate. When you study your mind you may find thoughts, as well as memories, that you had as a child. While many see thoughts, emotions, and experiences as different, there is no thought that is not attached to an emotion and no feeling that is not interconnected with a thought. Both affect the nature of our experiences. When we hold onto negative thoughts such as anger, bitterness, hatred, and jealousy they continue from the deeper levels of the mind to affect our surface thoughts and actions. They also have an effect on the body, distressing the immune system — just as expressing loving and positive thoughts strengthens the immune system. In time negative thoughts of depression, anger and hatred weaken the immune system and prevent it from properly fighting against diseases such as cancer, ulcers, etc.

DENIAL

When we label a thought as bad, we suppress it. We try to hide it from ourselves. We do mental hide-and-seek, pretending we didn't have unhappy, angry or hateful thoughts. In time and with practice, we can hide all sorts of destructive thinking. This is called denial. Often this thinking becomes self-destructive, because we cannot control all of our thinking. Suppressed negativity will creep into our day-to-day thoughts. We might suddenly become bitter or angry at times when we expect ourselves to be happy. For example after accomplishing something wonderful like birth, marriage, graduation, success at work, etc. We feel unfulfilled. Thus suppressed thoughts can be very unpredictable and uncontrollable. We may spend a lot of time trying to control compulsive re-emergence of negative thoughts.

One way to deal with this body of suppressed negative thoughts is to release them. In releasing them we can notice that we have angry, jealouse or malicious thoughts. When we release anger, we may feel antsy or upset, but we don't necessarily have to act on these old feelings and thoughts. Being relaxed helps us not to act upon every uncomfortable thought. We have come to understand that such thoughts may be normal and natural reactions to whatever is going on in our lives. We allow ourselves to have such thoughts/feelings for a moment. But we don't try to stop them from happening or from leaving. This is the way we learn not to obsess about negative thoughts, not to feel guilty or anxious, and not to deny them. Relaxation exercises such as Conscious Breathing (page 30) allow us to eventually let go of that suffering. When we are deeply relaxed and quiet, thoughts start coming to the surface of our mind. When we get in the habit of simply observing them, they quietly go away.

As we gain confidence in the process of releasing emotions and thoughts, we notice that our thinking patterns are converted from those of envy and fear to compassion for ourself and others. For the mind inevitably chooses one or the other. Letting the anger and anxiety pass, allows us to make room for solutions, for different ways of looking at the situation, and for positive and compassionate responses to ourselves, our experiences, and other people.

LEARNING TO BE WITHOUT THOUGHTS

We can learn to be without thoughts by taking a few minutes a day to reconfirm to ourselves that we do have the right to be. Below is an elaboration on the Conscious Breathing process in the chapter on exercises (see page 30). It is a practice that will also help you toward greater control over your "monkey mind," that part of the mind that thinks of everything under the sun rather than being still and relaxed. Take a moment and notice your breathing pattern when your mind is still. Then notice your breathing pattern when you are worrying or furious.

When we notice the rush of thoughts coming when we relax, in time, we will notice that the thoughts come in patterns. These patterns are connected to senstions in the body. Observing and letting go of sensations also releases thought patterns.

13. AWARENESS OF SENSATIONS

Eyes closed: Focus on your awareness. Allow your mind to be calm, peaceful, relaxed, and neutral. Become aware of the sensation around the breath through your nostriles. Then move your ability to be aware of sensations into your body and to the top of your head. Slowly and patiently move your awareness throughout your body. Become aware of each and every sensation. Is it an itching, tickly, pain, heavy, cold, warm, sharp, irritation, or any other sensation? See if you are aware of sensations on the inside of the body as well as the outside surfaces. You may encounter areas where you are unable to put your mental awareness, places where your mind just won't go, places where you almost go to sleep or you feel a fuzziness or cloudiness between your mind and your body. With time you will begin to be able to be aware of sensations everywhere in your body.

You may go through periods in which you feel that the sensations mean something, mean body problems. For the most part this is not the case as those sensations change in nature and location. As you observe and come back to a sensation, it may not be there or it may be an entirely different sensation. This mental inventory can help you become aware of physical problems before they become more apparent, as you learn to distinguish between sensations and your awareness of specific information in your body that points to illness. For most of us, our bodies are unknown. When I started such a practice, the idea of being mentally aware of my body was actually frightening.

When we notice sensations with a calm, peaceful, and neutral mind, it relaxes the body's various tensions, thus reversing processes that disrupt the body's functions. I have met people who have overcome serious illnesses with an ongoing use of Awareness of Sensations.

In time your awareness will change as you know your body on the most minute biochemical level, and ultimately on a universal level. This knowledge is not merely intellectual knowledge. Intellectually we tend to view our bodies as objects and relate to them as if we were outside of them. Awareness of all of our sensations, inch by inch, allows a complete experience of trust and confidence in our bodies. It puts us in charge or our health and our healing process. In control of our bodies, we are in control of our lives.

You may want to do the simpler Conscious Breathing Exercise (see page 30), for it can take hold in a few minutes. If you regularly can only do a few minutes a day, of either Conscious Breathing or Awareness of Sensations, you will change the quality of your life.

LONELINESS

We tend to identify this stillness with loneliness. Our fear of aloneness often keeps us from spending time with ourselves. It can drive us to fill that void with conquests, collections of friends, possessions, food, drugs, work, or belief systems. It is possible to see the stillness and the sense of essential aloneness as separate yet related experiences. First of all, the stillness can teach us again that we need only "be." If we need only "be" we do not need something to prove our right to exist. Of course we need nourishment and we are social by nature. But when we feel unworthy of mere existence, we are in terror whenever we are not doing something to justify our existence. We feel that being alone is evidence that somehow we have failed to prove that we have the right to "be." Thus aloneness is intolerable because it suggests human inadequacy.

BODY WISDOM

Various recently developed therapy processes such as the Hakomi method utilize the body's essential wisdom. How often have you had a gut feeling about something? As we develop ongoing conscious awareness of our bodies, we can use this "gut feeling" or essential wisdom to help us deal with problems or impending problems. This requires a fine-tuned body awareness. In the past I made a very serious error in not listening to my body. Everything was going wrong: the glands in my neck enlarged, I was limping and sweating, and I could not sleep at night. My physician could not make a diagnosis. Once the business crisis that my body had been trying to prevent occurred, all symptoms dissappeared. Had I realized that my body was trying to warn me, I would have listened and avoided the crisis.

14. BODY WISDOM

Put your attention within your body from time to time throughout the day. Make a mental note of various feelings in your body. Do you clench your teeth or your stomach? Do you feel queasy? Does your heart muscle tighten when certain things happen? Notice where the stresses are. Do your shoulders, back, or neck feel tightened or stressed? As you begin to learn where you put your stress, notice when and why you do so. Check out your body when you are upset, when you are frightened, when you are sad, when you are happy. Continue to make a mental inventory of the patterns in how your body reacts to your life. As you move through this process take times throughout the day to consciously relax the body by breathing or by noticing sensations. With an ongoing process of checking body reactions and relaxing the body you will begin to notice clear signs of your body trying to communicate with you, warning you about relationships, transitions, and decisions you may be about to make.

WE ARE AN ESSENTIAL PART OF THE UNIVERSE

In being still and alone with ourselves in the great stillness of the universe, in the following exercise we may be frightened at first. It means that we are part of it all. Somewhere in our past we had convinced ourselves that we were an exception in the universe. Somewhere perhaps we decided that we were so special as to be immortal and would not need to interact with life in ordinary ways. In realizing that we are another part of the universe, a part without which the universe would be incomplete, relax.

Children have had more recent experiences of their aloneness in the universe and of its great silence. Yet their very dependence upon adults for survival may seem to have invalidated this experience. Children often seem in a huge hurry to learn to be adults. Because they do not have our skills, when they see us hurrying and doing constantly, they may feel very inadequate to life. Giving them the gift of our quiet, and stillness lets them know that it is OK to just be.

---

15. EXPERIENCING MYSELF AS PART OF THE UNIVERSE

Go out into the night and look up at the stars.. Imagine yourself as part of this huge universe. Imagine yourself being as important as the brightest and most distant star or galaxy. Feel totally a part of the enormity of it, and part of the billions of years contained in it. See how you feel about this. What is going on with your heart? See yourself as small as the smallest atom. Notice when you feel tiny and when you feel huge. Why do you feel these things? Notice your feelings and ask yourself, "where do they come from and why do they occur?" You know the answer. Practice this often, and think of everyone on Earth watching this same sky with you.

TOUCH

Before you could talk, you were silent. Before you were born, you were silent. You may have heard many things and felt even more. You were keenly aware of your body. You were keenly aware of bodies that touched yours. Before you were born you knew your mother's body intimately. Every cell in your body knew every cell in her body. When you arrived in this world, you expected such intimacy. In response to this expectation of physical intimacy, you responded to touching. This is a reason for your thriving as a baby. Studies have shown that babies deprived of touch do not thrive nor do they grow normally. If you were fortunate, you were touched and held frequently and lovingly. Your memory, your ground of being is imprinted with this experience. An infant and child's experience of touch can imprint perfect acceptance. We can find our way toward using touch to create an experience of total acceptance in our adult life.

Unfortunately most schools have strong taboos against touch, often with good reasons. Physical aggression has often been expressed by children kicking, bitting, and hitting one another. Yet small children entering schools may have trouble dealing with a situations so alien to the intimacy created by touching at home. They may wish to touch other children as a sign of affection but find that those children come from homes with little touching. Both groups of children may have anxiety about touching. They may feel a great deal of confusion and loss. This confusion may lead children to try to act out their desire to be touched or their reaction to experiencing a strong but confusing taboo. I suspect this leads to much of the inappropriate physical behavior found in elementary schools. Sadly, this also creates a climate of estrangement among children because some children will engage in forms of permissable touching such as rough-housing, while other children look on and experience privation.

---

16. CUDDLING AND TOUCHING EXERCISE

This is appropriate for adults, parents and children. Take advantage of every opportunity to cuddle yourself and your children. But always with the permission and cooperation of the child or adult. Do not force physical contact upon another. Physical touch is important for children of all ages. If practiced early and continuously, it may be possible to be physically supportive of adults or children in this way. When reading stories or spending quiet, pleasurable time with yourself or with children make a cuddly nest, as warm and safe and secure as possible. Perhaps you will just sit there close to one another. Try to spend a large portion of the time just allowing yourself to be and to be close. Permit yourself to feel how it is to just be next to and touching another human without any other agenda. Make this a separate time from when you work out problems. Between adults, do not sexualize during this exercise. Adults need to learn to have physical intimacy free from sexual interaction. You may have signals that you create for one another that say this is to be a time for cuddling and nothing else.

The exercise below is also helpful to people who have received negative messages about touching, have been shamed about it. This powerful exercise permits people to have boundaries and also helps them deal with fears about touch. It is reassuring and supportive to have our boundaries acknowledged and respected. Children also need this respect. Often conflicts between children in schools can be attributed to violations of boundaries or a child's sense of integrity. It is important for teachers to recognize this and bring it out into the open. If adults tell children that they have the right to take care of themselves, we are giving them permission to take care of their lives. If, on the other hand, we ignore their desire to take care of their sense of integrity, we suggest that it is OK for others to violate that integrity as well.

17. BEING IN CONTROL OF BEING TOUCHED

This exercise is for adults and children who have been physically traumatized. Go very slowly. Ask permission to touch the other person. Ask exactly where, how, and what kind of touch the other wishes. Wait. Be very patient. Don't put any pressure on the other person. Allow the other to be completely in control throughout the experience. Repeating this often can be helpful for people who have been physically traumatized. Not wanting to be touched is OK. Honor this desire, too.

ADULT ANXIETIES ABOUT TOUCH

For adults touching is a complex issue. Reared in a world that abhors touch, we may be experiencing deep feelings of privation. We have deep terror of physical agression, and of uncontrolled sexuality. We have learned such fears from childhood onward. Many individuals and groups have communicated beliefs that touching, because of its possible connection to sexuality, particularly for older children, is basically bad and dangerous. It may take a long time for many adults to become reassured that touch is OK. In the meantime, the children in our lives experience our confusion.

18. TALKING ABOUT TOUCH

Appropriate for adolescents for whom touch is taboo and for adults who fear or are apprehensive about touch. Talk about touching. How does it feel to be touched or to touch another? What do you want from touching and being touched? Why? How much? How do you respond to touching or being touched? When deprived, how do you feel? Where and when do you feel the need for touching?

Teachers and parents should start working with these issues as quickly as possible — by talking about it and finding ways to support our human need for touch — so that children are not forced to suppress their need for touch. When touch issues are ignored, the end result may be early sexual expeiences where sex becomes an illicit behavior or a violent outburst.

19. CREATING RULES FOR TOUCHING

If K-3 teachers are permitted and wish to, they can create a set of signals or verbal statements that help the children in that classroom know that it OK to be touched. Children can learn to communicate that they like to be touched or that they wish to touch another child. Each child can establish his or her own parameters for touching. The group can talk about respecting another child's touch boundaries. If children are permitted to say what touching they do not like then they will monitor what is OK and what is not OK. Be cautious when dealing with children who are confused about this. Teachers may monitor the quality of the touching without terminating physical contact or suggesting that touching is bad. In addition, they can help children learn to be assertive monitors of what kind of touching they wish to allow for themselves and from themselves. Be aware of physical contact between children.

This exercise builds a child's sense of boundaries, and may help him to get needed physical affection. Remember, babies fail to thrive without touch. Even elderly who have pets or people in their lives to touch and be touched by are much healthier than those who live in isolation. This information about touch suggests that the more touch-oriented we are, the better our emotional and physical health.

20. OBSERVING OUR RELATIONSHIP TO OUR BODIES

Observe infants and small children. See how they deal with their bodies. Notice that they may actually see their bodies as something they have, not as something they are. Now observe older children. Notice the change in how they are with their bodies. Now observe adults. Notice how adults deal with their bodies. Did you notice the way adults relate to their bodies? Do some act in a way that will deny that the body is there, that they are sexual, or that they are mortal? Notice adults who are at ease with their bodies.

As we interact more closely with each other's bodies, we become more aware of our own mortal body. We may fear for our safety and survival; this belief/experience/consciousness is reinforced by those with whom we physically interact. Society attempts to deny bodies, to reduce them to odorless, blemishless, thin, and highly controlled ideals. If we do not touch other people, we won't be reminded of our own bodies, of their supposed inadequacies. Often we are extremely critical of our physical appearances. However, we may also look for proof that somehow we are an exception to the nature of bodies, that our body won't die and decay. Behind the drive for physical perfection often lurks a denial of the uniqueness and impermanence of a body. Have you noticed how narrowly we define physical health and physical beauty? The term "flawless" often is associated with beauty, as if flaws are hints of things to come. Flawed bodies can betray people, just as flawed lives do. Learning to touch one another in nonsexual ways can help us reach an intimacy and sense of caring beyond our fear about our own essential aloneness and mortality. This may not make sense to our intellectual mind, but parts of us knows that this is so. Being touched with boundary sensitivity and awareness makes us less preoccupied with the body's importance, and enhances feeling closeness with the "beingness" beyond the body.

If parents can maintain a way of comforting and showing physical intimacy, it may help maintain closeness even in the push-away phases of early adolescence. The following exercise helps adults explore and become aware of lost experiences and feelings about physical intimacy. Again, this book and these exercises are about self-esteem and children. However occassional exercises for adults only will appear to help adults work on material which may impinge upon their relationship with children. Children do not develop their individuality and sexuality in physical interaction with their caregivers. They need the safety of parental care and compassion. A child's safety is at risk when the very powerful adult ego involvement of sex enters into an activity. Nearly all adults have unresolved ego needs and compulsions around sex. We adults need to work these issues out on our own: it is the proper provenance of another book on adult sexuality and self-esteem.

This exercise helps adults see how they feel about their bodies. It is important that adults are clear about their body issues before interacting with children on self-esteem and touch issues.

21. CONTROLLED TOUCHING (ADULTS)

With another trustworthy and caring adult, work with the following instructions. This is not a sexual exercise. Have the other adult touch you. Vary the touch as your inner feelings guide you. Simply notice what feelings come up. Try not to talk about them until you are finished interacting. Experiment with all sorts of touching: simply laying a hand on, brushing up against another, caressing, hugging, and so forth. Trade off touching and being touched. Let all of the feelings that come up work their way through you. You may do this exercise regularly and will find you may work through very powerful feelings. Stop the work if it becomes too intense and come back to it at another time.

Possibly you will recall times as a child in which you had a great need to be touched and reassured. Over time you will be able to bring back all sorts of emotions and experiences from your past which you have stored within your body. You will find in the subtlety of touch the unlocking of complex personal memories.

ADULT SEXUALIZING OF TOUCH

Many adults answer the desire for intimacy the only way that they know — by sexualizing touch. Often they sexualize to such a degree that they cannot experience physical intimacy, but only the anxiety around sexuality. Thus the anxiety about not having touch in their lives is compounded with the performance anxiety related to sex. It is important that we untangle these two sets of feelings so that we distinguish between intimacy and sexual intimacy. Adults need to work toward clearing up this confusion or they will pass it on to their children.

CONFUSION ABOUT TOUCHING
IN CONTEMPORARY SOCIETY

I was recently at a high school where if a teacher so much as touched a student on the wrist, there was talk of a law suit. The teachers and students were apparently in a power struggle that surfaced as a detente around the issue of touch. In some instances teachers have abused their relationship with a child, acted out his/her own sexual needs, or physically punished a child. We are no more than a couple of decades from a time in which corporal punishment was considered OK and necessary for classroom discipline. In these changing and confusing times there is still little clarity about touching and being touched by other people, particularly by nonrelatives. We know a great deal of sexual and physical abuse of children goes on among families and between unrelated people. While such violations have only recently been recorded, the problem is old. We may be at a period in time in which we will do more talking about touching than actually touching. But talking can help people establish their limits, what they want, and how they will relate to the wants of others. Deep within each of us is still the need to be touched. Touching moves us closer, an act of others accepting us more completely. While all true joining is of the mind, so often there is an intellectual distance of judgement and rejection. Touching often breaks through this distance.

STORING EMOTIONS IN THE BODY

Often, where we store strong feelings and traumas in the body becomes a location for chronic conditions or diseases. Every cell in our body is intelligent. Each contains the primary forms of intelligence in the DNA, and cells are connected to the nervous system, the communication system for intelligence. People are suprised when they first discover feelings in their body at great distances from the mind. Massage can trigger these feelings. The term "emotional bodywork" applies to the technique used by massage therapists who are trained in counseling. When a body memory is released, usually during deep-tissue work, the therapist works with the client to explore and let go of the emotional memory.

In Western society, we do not learn much about the feelings we have stored in our bodies. This learning would bring us into greater intimacy and acceptance of our own bodies. This information could be very helpful to children whose bodies change so dramatically as they mature. To know that their growing and changing bodies are intelligent and responsive to what happens helps adolescents feel more in control.

KNOW YOUR BODY

Learn about your own body. Know its cycles, its ups and downs. Accept it as it is, knowing that several billion different and unique bodies live in this world. Each is supremely fitted to the person who wears it. Compassion toward your own body will help you deal with the changes it goes through. During childhood we go through the greatest degree of physical change. It often can be baffling, frightening, and emotionally painful. When adults intellectualize this, (i.e. relate it to an intellectual problem with clear solutions), this lack of body awareness is passed on to the children. Children do not know who to go to to get "real" information. Children go to other children for information about their bodies, and it's no wonder they enter adult life with confusing information. We have ritualized this approach in education. Our so-called health units rarely allow children to discuss their bodies but instead give scientific theories of the body "safe" for adults but useless for children.

Just at a time when children need to trust and accept their bodies, they are given a frame work in academic education that expects them to control themselves. Intellectual approaches tend to give the illusion of control. They postulate rules and regulations. They suggest a static world devoid of emotions. A process orientation rooted firmly in experience and the understanding of how the body is and how it changes from day to day, minute to minute, offers children a perspective on their own struggle to understand and cope with their bodies. This is particularly crucial in adolescence.

---

22. A BODY JOURNAL

Keep a personal journal, biography in which you keep track of your body. Record everything. Take an inventory of your body. Where is it at this age as compared to another age? Children can make an inventory of growth and changes, keeping track of weight and height as well as other bodily changes. This is a private journal, with scrupulous integrity and intimacy restrictions. Notice your patterns of concern. Notice different types of concerns that you have with your body. With each entry make a goal to accept your body. Accept all of what you consider to be its failures and flaws. Accept its good qualities. Find ways to love and trust your body. Allow this love to flourish and bloom.

Our society focuses upon the perfect body. By the time children reach 12 years of age this "perfect body" has impact upon the child's own body image. Adults can counter this narrow view by becoming aware of the diversity of bodies. Talk about how wonderful it is to live in a world where there are so many different possible bodies, faces, and ways of dressing. Our society contains a vast array of minorities from every corner of the world.

23. MY BODY SELF-IMAGE

(For adults, and parents. Often by seven or eight, children are so self-conscious that this may also be a painful exercise for them.) Stand in front of the mirror. Look at yourself. See all of the parts of yourself. Speak aloud or inside of yourself of your acceptance of each and every part and detail of your body. Work consciously toward loving how your body is. Breathe through your resistance to looking at certain parts. When you feel negative thoughts about your body, breathe and become conscious of your breathing. Let go of those thoughts. Bring your attention back to that part of the body and find a way to see it as wonderful.

24. POSITIVE BODY SELF-IMAGE

(You can do this exercise with children of all ages. Try doing it eyes-closed with guidance in which children are asked to see themselves in their mind's eye. Use these statements to guide others when looking at their own bodies. Then use them when looking at the bodies of others): "This is the body of a wonderful person. This body is whole and complete and perfect as it is. I do not need to change it. He/she does not need to change it at all. My body is growing and evolving so that it can support me in doing all of the things that I am doing. I like my body. I take very good care of it. I have reverence for my body and the bodies of others. I do not do anything to harm my body or to harm the bodies of other people. It is fun to be in my body, I can do all sorts of fun things like....."

COMMUNICATION AND THE BODY

When your world was silent or limited by your language skills, you learned to read, to feel, and to experience the people around you through your physical experiences. You learned to look for clues from the gathering tension in a parent's face, their anxious movements, or your parent's fights. You smelled them, and you smelled the changes within the household. You felt the tension as a palpable experience as well as the joy and release. When you lay against your mother or father, you felt her or his body. A part of your intelligence, developed while you were in your mother's womb, knows her moods, her rhythms, and the biochemical changes that accompany her every moment. Memory within the cells of your body has record of your physical universe.

---

25. BLINDFOLDED AWARENESS

For a group of adults, or adults and children, or children and children. Do this exercise in a park, a yard, or a garden. At school, consider a courtyard or play area. Divide into partners and blindfold one. The other partner leads the blindfolded one around. Guiding her/him through all sorts of experiences. Touch things: grass, walls, objects, water. The leader finds different textures and sensations: cold, warm, prickly,etc. Smell things: flowers, people, animals, inside buildings, outside, etc. Hear things: running water, the breeze, rain, birds, insects, silence, the footsteps you make, etc. Switch with the other partner wearing the blindfold. Talk about this exercise when you are finished.

This exercise helps to bring us back to that time when we were dependent, when intelligence was focused upon the most subtle nuances of external information. This game is especially helpful in developing trust. It can be used to create trust within a groups of children working on a project. Each person participates and shares the dependency experience. It can be most helpful with adolescents, particularly if younger children are mixed in. When blindfolded, we can regain experiences of being in tune with another person's movement, intentions, and the flow of the world around us, (like the child in the womb). We draw on an emmense range of sensory data.

BODY LANGUAGE

When watching body language, you are incorporating all sorts of sensory information. You can, in fact, smell other people, though that smell is not as keen as it is with other animals. We can smell fear, happiness, or anger, suffering, etc. In the chapter on listening, we will discuss how finely tuned our ears are to hear the nuances of voices. As a child, you heard keenly because your survival depended more upon it. We can also feel the energy of other people consciously or not. When we feel this energy, we may act upon it. Many of us have had the experience of being with a child who totally changes behavior when entering a situation with a different group of people. Some children will be very calm and quiet with one person and very excited with another.

During the Blindfold Exercise you may be able to feel your partner's energy or emotional quality, and perhaps even know in advance what he or she will do. We are not solid forms but in fact energy patterns, first and foremost. As we become quiet and alert, we experience all sorts of energy patterns. Small children are still accustomed to experiencing energy patterns. Knowing their parents moods not only from the expressions on their faces but also from feeling the parent's energy pattern. Is the parent scattered and feeling out of control? This maybe the moment that a child will try to take advantage of the parent's disaray. How many times have the children in your life asked for things when you were feeling particularly distracted or upset? Children are geniuses at seizing these moments.

MIXED SIGNALS

As we grow up we find that adults give us mixed signals. Adults offer children contradicting information. Often the words adults say do not correspond to tone of voice, smells, physical gestures, nor to the energy patterns. We say, "Do your homework." but our body language lacks conviction. We may be remembering what a crushing burden homework felt like when we were children. If adults reinforce contradicting communication through exertion of power, the child distrust information he gets. He will decide not to trust what his eyes tell him and his body feels. This can lead to disastrous experiences in which children trust adults who are only interested in using the child for their own needs, often sexual or violent needs. So it is in every adult's best interest to honor the child's ability to read or experience all sorts of forms of communication.

WATCHING FOR SIGNALS

Adults have extensive knowledge of what various body expressions, postures, and interconnections mean. Because we learned these signals when our own ability to communicate was limited, we have internalized all sorts of reactions to them. All sorts of feelings come up when we experience them. We often have not sorted out all of the responses that our mind and body make. Our minds are moving through personal catalogues of memories of sound, smell, hearing, checking this experience against our current feelings and thoughts and the emotions and beliefs of others. We try to interact with the world using this incredibly complex information. We want to do the right thing, to minimize our suffering and increase our pleasure and happiness. Sometimes this means that we over-anticipate, trying to prevent unforseeable disasters. Often we have uncomfortable feelings based on our experience of this complex set of signals. But we have lost our capacity to decode them. What are the signals telling us? As we learn to value and utilize this complex, yet subtle, basic knowledge, we can act with clarity and decisiveness. Many call this intuition. It is simply paying attention to the thousands of signals within, which constantly communicate. At times I get a strong feeling to do or not to do something. I have found that when I heed these feeling I avoid problems, and when I ignore them I don't.

FOR CHILDREN, INTUITION IS KNOWLEDGE

The younger the child the more he is used to feeling and sensing everything in his world. As the child slowyly puts on the layers of verbal communication, his non-verbal awareness drops below the level of conscious communication. This does not mean that the experiences go away. Information from knowledge of the nonverbal world is a constant, and his body responds to what he intuits. Responding to fears and anxieties, he acts out this awareness. He may run wildly for no apparent reason or start a fight or break toys. We cannot see why. His mind is telling him to get away, to get control over others, or to make people notice his feelings. A child's body responds to longings, joys, and a myriad of other experiences.

The child collects and interacts with information, integrating it into his own processes. This is not primitive information. It is part of the basis for his creative leaps, for his future drive and greatness. The mass of this learning is much greater than any he will derive from books or conversations. It helps him to weave his way through society, to find groups and individuals with which to interact, to follow life goals and purposes, to organize his body for various activities. A child utilizes this massive information to learn to walk and talk. It is critical at every step in his growth and learning. This is the very foundation upon which a child's existence rests. Adults can assist a child by validating this information whenever a child brings it to the surface and wishes to talk about it. They can also help him become conscious of how this process works, how he finds his way, makes his choices between different behaviors, different possibilities.

Classrooms, Kindergarten through Second grade, are beginning to acknowledge the foundation of understanding in nonverbal experience by their mutilevel, multiseonsory approach to learning. This approach needs to extend throughout the grades. We can all extend our knowledge of ourselves by observing the nonverbal organization of the world around us.

26. AWARENESS OF BODY LANGUAGE

Make a log of nonverbal communication around you. How do people sit? How do they stand? How do they use their bodies to interact with other people? How does this body language vary according to the power and status, age and sex of the person with whom they are interacting? What are the facial expressions? What is the quality of energy? Is it anxious? Excited? Nervous? Slow and depressed? Is it relaxed? Notice how you respond to these observations. Now make a log of how you hold you body and the energy you feel as you interact with different people.

OUR BODY LEARNED TO BE PART OF THE FAMILY OF OUR ORIGIN

Children learned to walk, talk, and respond just like other family members. A boy may walk just like his father. A child naturally and spontaneously incorporates family ways of understanding. Virginia Satir's work with families analyzed how we organize our bodies during psychological interactions with one another — how the psychological feels. We have grown and shaped our bodies under direction from our minds as well as our genes. This bodily growth is influenced by how we feel and fit into our families. We hold our bodies upright, the tensions in our organs and muscles, even the way our bones are held in place, is a product of what we learned from our family. This can be passed on from generation to generation. My sisters and I have the same verbal tone and emotion to our voices, just as our uncles on our mother's side all laughed alike. Virginia Satir gives the family a concrete sense of its dynamic by arranging the members into physical patterns. I observed such a pattern in a "family reconstruction" by one of Satir's associates that struck me on a very visceral level as being true of the painful balance of my own family experience. Families often displace member's sense of inner balance and harmony by distorting individuals in order to give the out-of-control family a sense of balance.(1.)

When we're conscious of our inner selves, both physically and emotionally, we begin to correct any inbalances we may have created. Being aware in itself can reverse much of this, along with releasing the feelings and memories held in the body and the mind. Conversely we can often change our whole approach to life by readjusting the body's inner dynamic.

The work of great thinkers comes from the integration of all aspects of understanding, verbal and nonverbal. Einstein suddenly understood the nature of relativity as he stood at a street crosswalk in Switzerland. As he walked down the street, and waited at the intersection, he triggered a thought process about the nature of the universe. His whole body participated in the movement of his intuition and thinking processes within the different levels of his consciousness.

MIND BODY

Breakthoughs in art or music or science come from the sudden convergence of a complex inner consciousness, including the knowledge locked in our body awareness. If we are too busy and noisy, we do not notice our stream of intelligence that lies beneath the surface. Despite the misperceptions in our intellectual sense of ourselves that suggest that we are lacking, inadequate, incapable, our bodies will often tell us the truth. We know what's right for us, but often our fears will fool us. Our bodies retain our original perfection as humans and can carry us across burning hot coals in a firewalk. They are connected with our deepest ground of being. Our bodies can heal themselves of cancers and other serious diseases. They are connected to our source of genius.

GAMES AND EXERCISES
TO RESTORE OUR NONVERBAL AWARENESS

Children love to play games. Divide them into teams and let them each take a turn. When I play this sort of game with children, I rank the levels of understanding. So, complicated gestures are worth (3) points, and simple ones are (1) point. One by one, each person from alternating teams is a mime. If players guess correctly then the mime's team gets points. Children love to play games that demand thinking and creativity. In the process they learn about themselves.

27. MIMING GESTURES AND EXPRESSIONS

(For children and adults.) Before a group mime all sorts of gestures. Make a list of possible gestures, expressions, and body language in advance. Have the participants guess what is going on. See if you can come as close as possible to various physical expressions of moods, emotions, and thoughts that you have experienced in your own life. Types of gestures or body postures: accusing, comforting, fear, dissappointment, torn up, twisted in knots, worried, suffering, happy, relaxed, and so forth. Take turns being the mime. Now go out and observe people's body language. Come back and try again. To adapt this exercise as a game, have the audience guess what is going on after the performance has taken place.

28. TALKING ABOUT BODY LANGUAGE

(For children and adults) After miming body language, and observation talk about what body language means to us. Talkabout how it felt when you expressed various mental states with your body. Bring nonverbal communication to conscious discussion. Even the youngest children know a lot about what is going on nonverbally.

Footnote:
(1.) Satir, Virginia; The New Peoplemaking, Science and Behavior Books, Inc., Mountain View, 1988.

5. LISTENING

As infants, our whole intelligence is at first directed toward the world just next to us, the world of smell, and touch, and energy, and feelings. After we learn to experience silence we learn to listen. We hear the texture and nature of relationships. As infants and small children, we pay close attention because our whole existence and survival depend upon what we hear.

---

29. LISTEN TO YOUR CHILDHOOD

Go back to the time when you were a child. See yourself clearly as you were at any point in your childhood. Try to visualize this as clearly as you can. Now listen. Try to hear what you heard then. Get in touch with the smells, the feelings of the day. The feelings in your body, your thoughts, and your experience of that moment. As you do this exercise, over time re-create the various periods in your life. They are all there within you: the excitement, wonder, and pain of your childhood. They are part physical, emotional, and verbal. See if, when you recall sounds, you feel things in your body.

From the very beginning, even before they know the words, children know the difference between what is being said and what is being felt. Sounds are often stronger keys to our feelings than are visual cues. In the adult world, we can see enormous gaps between the words and the feelings behind them. Families have voice patterns. About 12 years ago I became aware that emotion had been deadened in my voice, expressing the level of my emotional shut down. In a sense, my shut down was hidden from me but others sensed it in my voice. As I have worked upon being honest about my feelings, my voice has gained emotion.

Children can hear adults say "I love you," with honesty, out of the deepest part of themselves. Or they can hear sentiments of love expressed with hatred and anger, or with disparagement and despair. Thousands of variations of feelings are placed upon a simple statement made within a child's hearing range. Ways in which we say "I love you" or any other communication can tinge the statement and make hearing it incredibly complex and confusing to children. If our voices carry confusing and contradictory deeper feelings, then the person who hears has to decide whether to respond to what the words say or what they sense beneath the words. Children, especially tend to take responsibility for their world and what goes on long before they understand their actual position in it. Thus emotional content and words can be conflicting and painful. Such confusion can cause children to shut down valid and vital emotional responses to communication quite early.

Do the following exercise observing children. Next do it observing the child part of adults. See if you can observe old traces of different stages of childhood in adults.

---

30. LISTEN TO A CHILD

Listen to children closely. Pay attention to everything that is going on. Hear the emotional quality. Notice the emotional quality of that child's communication and how it relates to that of other children and of the adults around the child. See if you can notice the connections between people through the quality of emotion being communicated - not just by facial expression, body language, and words, but particularly by the voice. Check your childhood memories, see if you notice any connections.

CHILDREN LEARN ABOUT THEMSELVES FROM WHAT THEY HEAR

Day by day a child learns from what he hears, and this forms an important part of the foundation of a child's view of himself and of the world. Helping him learn the tools for sorting out and using this learning to strengthen his positive self-concept would seem the logical use of our relationship with him. In order to do this we need to give him time, energy, and elbow room in which to sort it all out and integrate any new emotional information as well as intellectual information. We need to have feedback in order to understand exactly how he is perceiving his world. To do this we must know ourselves. Otherwise, we may be too consumed by our defenses and interpretations of events to hear a child's. We need to learn to listen and observe from the child's specific and personal point of view. Listening is an underestimated skill in dealing with children.

---

31. WHAT ARE WE HEARING?
WHAT ARE WE SAYING?

When you are in a situation or conversation in which you can simply listen, notice the following. What is the other person saying? What are you saying? What do you think is really being said, underneath this? What are your responses, in your body, in your feelings, to what is being said? What do you think about that person? What do you think is revealed about him/her in what is being said? What do you think is being revealed about you in your interpretations of what the other person is saying? What outcome do you want to this insight? What insight did your gain about conversations?

Variation: Listen without talking. See how you feel about the act of listening. See how your capacity to hear is affected by your decision not to talk. Notice how much you can hear in the process of communication, not simply in the words being said but the whole complex of feelings and intentions.

If you listen to yourself carefully you will hear yourself, not just what you are saying but how your mind is interacting with other people. Now listen to others speak, to people whom you consider insignificant, listen to children, listen to people you think are more important (authorities, or powerful figures). Notice your different thought responses, and body and emotional responses. Watch to see if your voice sounds different when talking to people who you fear or respect. If you can let go your interior mental activity, you can improve your capacity to hear what others are saying and why they are saying it. Listen with an open heart and an open mind. You know how to do this. You learned how when you were listening as a child.

NONINTERACTIVE COMMUNICATION

Much adult child communication is top down, chain of command. Under these circumstances adults often do not listen to or hear the child. Education often focuses upon the perfectionism of acceptable answers to programmed questions. "What is this?" If instead of telling a parent exactly what it is — say a water spot — the child starts to tell the parent all sorts of things about her feelings, thoughts, and learning, the parent or teacher may become impatient. The adult may have an agenda for asking the question. Perhaps they find the water annoying: the child has made a mistake. Or perhaps they want to know if the child will be able to tell them when they want a drink of water, etc. Perhaps the child's verbal skills are limited and she cannot clearly explain what she wants to tell us about the water. Sometimes adults are "on automatic" and aren't really paying attention. Learning to listen is learning to be aware, to be consciously present at communication. For nothing tells a child that they matter more than for adults to be consciously there for children.

Again, this is all applicable in our relationships with other adults. We often re-enact old conversations rather than actually listening to what is going on. So great is our anxiety and desire to anticipate disaster that we react before we have to.

LISTENING IS CRITICAL IN LEARNING READINESS

I have a one-and-a-half-year-old grandchild who interacts with me in very intelligent conversations, despite his limited vocabulary. We talk about birds, and he is quite aware of the different kinds of birds. Ever since he had a bird eat out of his hands, he is always on the lookout for birds. He tells me by putting his palm upward and wiggling his fingers as if to beckon birds toward him. I can only guess that seeing the birds come down and eat was wonderful for him. He is ready to learn about the wildness and sense of freedom that birds have. It is a great lesson because it is also about his integrity. I will soon see it when he becomes a fantasy personality, putting on a Batman cape and running around with the freedom of the birds. Each child has a great knowledge of his own world. He is not a categorical child but an actual and specific child, a person.

Try to give children an algebra lesson before they have learned the idea of making a symbol mark stand for a number of different things. The children will simply become confused and the lesson takes forever. Learning comes in steps, first simple numbers, then letters that stand for numbers, etc. Children know an enormous amount, specifically and personally. It makes a great deal of sense to fit new information into the pattern already established by the child's understanding. That way it will make sense to him and he will easily accept it and incorporate it into his ongoing life. However, we cannot do that unless we know his level of understanding. It may seem simpler just to ignore that level and pour or force the information into him. We like the idea of uniformity of teaching and learning because it seems more equal and fair. In the long run, it fails; with some exceptions, as children develop their personalities, they become more and more resistant to our attempts to force them to "learn" when they are not ready or when the feel they have no control over the process. This is why imposed learning becomes an incredibly inefficient practice.

HEARING IS CENTRAL TO RECEIVING FEEDBACK

Feedback learning is specific to a child's understanding and not simply a repetitive spitting back of programmed information. Feedback learning occurs when the teacher knows exactly what the child's capacity is and organizes information to match that specific child's place in his own learning process. When feedback learning becomes more prevalent in education, schools will be powerful and effective in using the genius with which children learn to walk and talk. I have a great deal of sympathy, for parents and teachers who are doing what was done with them, often in conditions which would overwhelm the average human. This is what these parents and teachers know to do. But if we can invent intelligence in computers, we can create new ways of interacting with children in order to support their personal growth and learning.

MIRRORING

Central to learning to listen is learning to reflect what is being said. This cuts down on the time necessary for people to explain and re-explain. Even if another is communicating in a confused manner, i.e. he says words that don't match his feelings, we can help sort out what he is trying to communicate by mirroring the communication. To develop listening skills it is helpful to learn to mirror another person. Children love to do this fun game in which they can act in many ways and the other person follows them. This is a warm up for active listening.

---

32. REFLECTIONS IN A MIRROR

Pretend a mirror is between you and another person, and one of you is the reflection. You can sit down or stand up to do this. The reflection attempts to do and say everything that the other person says or does. Take turns.

BEING COMPLETELY HEARD

Children and adults need to be heard. Whatever they are saying is of utmost importance to them. That is why it is so important to be completely aware and "there" in interactions, even if children are simply talking about experiences at play. If our minds are wandering or obsessing, we can't be "there." Virginia Satir calls acknowledging precisely what we hear: "mirroring." Mirroring means to children that their communications are heard, and that their deepest needs and feelings are accepted as valid by the another. Whether adults can deal with everything at that moment is of far less importance than for a child to know that the adult heard him. This process is also vital to adults. Active listening can help individuals work through most issues. We all want to know that we have been heard and understood. We don't want to feel that we are invisible.

33. MIRRORING 2: ACTIVE LISTENING

One person is the talker and the other is the listener. The listener listens carefully to what the other person has to say. Then the listener retells the other person what he or she has heard. The listener should try not to add anything of his or her own to what he retells. This is not mimicry or a precise reflection, but a conscious act of completely understanding what the other person is saying. The listener's job is to learn to tell the other what he or she has said, and let the other person know that the listener has heard the communication completely, thoroughly, and on the deepest possible level. This is a process of accepting the other person. Not of correcting, teaching, or arguing with the other person. See how closely you can mirror both the feelings and the communication. When you are through, discuss how it felt. Let the talker tell how it felt to be heard. Have the listener talk about how it felt to listen. Now change sides. Let the talker listen and the listener talk. Again, discuss how this felt when you have finished.

34. MIRRORING 3

Mirror a child. Take time to interact with a child in such a way that you add nothing of your own opinions, beliefs, attitudes, or even thoughts. Let the child tell you whatever he or she wishes. Make minimal responses that keep the process going. This will take much practice. It will be rewarding in that you will begin to gain insight into the wisdom that children have despite their age.

35. OBSERVATIONS OF MIRRORING

Observe yourself interacting with others. Notice how you feel if people try to judge, correct, and help you make decisions about what you are telling them. Now notice how you feel when another person simply listens to you and encapsulates what you have been saying.

As we acknowledge the suffering and the joy of the child or adult, they can release it. They no longer need to keep it hidden away from others, out of a sense of shame or fear of rejection.

Even if he has made a mistake and is communicating bad behavior, a neutral person — child or adult — mirroring the child can
help the child acknowledge his mistake and find the means to correct it. The child struggles with finding meaning or a way of
dealing with cruelty and irrationality in the world around him. If we
can be as neutral as possible when acknowledging what he is
communicating, we allow the child to use us to sort out what he
is feeling, what experiences are his and which belong to others,
and what is his relative position in the situation. He is sorting
out his inner map of consciousness and restoring his image of
himself as a valuable and positive contributor to society.

Mirroring is almost like a dance in which the listener follows. It
may be difficult as so many of us have felt neglected and want to
have others pay attention to them. When we learn the mirroring
dance, we may also find more people willing to mirror us, and our
compulsive need to be the center of attention will disappear.

LISTENING TO OUR INTUITION

Listening is one half of verbal communication. Listening is an
important development in one's self-esteem, for it means that one
is ready to receive. This is very helpful in receiving communication from deep within oneself as well. For our inner feelings may
often be overwhelmed by a noisy world outside. As we develop
our capacity to listen, we come to hear very quiet feelings and
thoughts within. Hearing what goes on within helps us to stay connected with our deepest purposes in being on this planet. It allows
us to utilize the tremendous power and energy coming from
being connected with our highest or most evolved purposes.
Our busy mind may draw us away and focus upon the short
term — our impatience and anxiety about our survival. Listening
means we can be quiet and hear everything that is to be heard
from any moment or communication. You'll find a multitude of
meanings in the most innocent of communications.

THE WONDER CHILD

Artists often use the wonder child as a source of their creativity. When painting, composing, or writing it has been the source
of their brilliance and genius. Genius is prevalent in everyone. I
want the children in my life to be the greatness that they have the
potential to be, don't you?

Guided processes such as these are multipurpose. A Breathing Exercise (page 30) or music will help participants relax and become comfortable and safe. Before starting the following process, adults may direct it toward a goal they or the child envisions. It is very powerful in putting children in touch with their inner-most self-knowledge. Teachers and parents should be leery of violating the child's personal views. A teacher can use the process to communicate about goals in the classroom in as much as they are congruent with a child's own positive self-image. The child will create his own vision of how it is. The power comes from his capacity to feel control over the vision. It is his being that he sees, not one we have fabricated for him.

---

36. INNER TALK - GUIDED EXERCISE

(This may be done with either children or adults.) See yourself walking along a brook or a beautiful place with water and nature all around you. You hear the sounds of nature, the birds, the water moving, the wind blowing softly against your skin. You feel very peaceful and happy. Now you see someone coming toward you. You see that it is your Wonder Child. Your Wonder Child comes up to you, he/she smiles. he/she is very happy to see you, is confident, and filled with peace. He/she leans over and whispers something to you. (Stop the guidance for a while so that the Wonder Child can whisper something.) You talk to each other. You are very glad to see your Wonder Child. You tell him/her "good bye." He/she turns and walks away. You feel very happy and peaceful. You keep the secret you shared with your Wonder Child close to your heart.

KEEPING YOUR SPECIAL PLACES AND FEELINGS TO YOURSELF

It is best not to have children talk about this vision because they are quite vulnerable to the invalidation of one another. Let the child keep this secret, until he feels he wants to share it.

LEARNING TO BE QUIET

In chapter two we had many exercises to learn to quiet our mind. The following exercises allow us to use this quiet to hear beyond what we normally hear.

---

37. LISTEN TO YOUR QUIETNESS

Close your eyes or keep them open as you wish. Listen to yourself. Listen to your thoughts. Listen to your body. Listen to your feelings. Now see if you can hear, feel, or experience quietness deep inside of you. See what it is like. See how long you can experience it. See what happens as you are experiencing it. Do your feelings interrupt? Does your body make a lot of noise? What happens? How does it feel to hear your quietness?

LISTEN TO THE UNIVERSE

Listening is a skill whose dimensions and potential have only been lightly touched. Training ourselves to listen and to hear helps us begin to notice and see beyond our personal limits. Training our children to listen is training them to be visionaries. They will be able to utilize that power to transform their lives and solve problems on planet Earth. We can give them skills which to help them solve the problems: we can empower our children while we empower ourselves.

---

38. LISTEN TO THE UNIVERSE

Be quiet and listen. Try to listen beyond the confines of your own mind, beyond your body. Try to listen beyond the birds, the wind, and the sounds of the world outside of you. Notice if you can hear the vastness of the universe. Listen beyond the limits of your hearing. You may begin to notice that you can develop subtleties in your capacity to hear and grow in your ability to understand what you are hearing.

What did Beethoven, who was deaf, hear as he composed his last symphony? While this may seem a far out exercise, it is intended to stretch your limits. It takes our capacity to experience and be aware beyond what we have known so far. All of the exercises in this and other chapters can also do this. With repetition they will support the evolution of our awareness capacity, creativity, and genius.

6. TALKING

If we could remember when we first learned to talk we would know how to better rear and interact with our own children. Talking is one of the most comprehensive and intellectually challenging things we humans learn to do. Yet nearly every child learns to talk. When she learns her oral language she also learns thousands of inflections of meaning, some of it cultural and some familial. She learns what words such as "negro," "money," and "love" mean. A meaning deeply rooted in her culture and family. All of these meanings are surrounded by a world of unexpressed or partially expressed feelings and beliefs. A child works toward putting herself into words, seeing herself as part of this language of meanings.

Adults want their children to see themselves as having the power and ability to deal with language. But they also want language to serve rather than enslave. The language children use in describing themselves, in talking about their lives, often tells us how they think about themselves. It tells us whether they are empowered in life or feel diminished and have a poor self-image as a result of their interactions with us and their culture.

LEARNING TO COMMUNICATE
IN A NURTURING ENVIRONMENT

My child learned to talk in the same way she learned to walk, in an informal and highly personal way. She learned at her own speed and, to a high degree, in her own way. She learned by testing, experimenting, and repetition. Generally in learning to walk and talk, children are brilliant students. But when they are distressed by problems in their life they can stop the process, go backward or not embark upon it. I have been in many special education classrooms where children struggle to learn these essential skills, children who are often without apparent physical handicap. I believe that often the parents are doing their best. These experiences demonstrate the fragility of a child's sense of well-being and power over her life and experiences. And how important optimal conditions are to any learning process. As natural as walking and talking seem, they flourish in a nurturing environment, one which supports a child's self-esteem.

74 TALKING

Imagine how it felt when you learned your first few words. How exciting it was. How you might have thought to yourself, "At last I am going to tell these wonderful and powerful beings, my parents and the others in my life, what exactly has been going on with me since I was born. Now I'm going to get to tell them exactly what I think about what is happening to me." I see this expression on the faces of the infants and toddlers in my life, at the point of their first words. Of course a child spends years of learning her language before she has the fluency to tell these things. In the meantime she has gotten use to talking about the world with her personalized vocabulary and has formed viewpoints.

By the time she goes to school, our child has learned thousands of words. She has learned about all sorts of cultural road signs like "Big Bird" and "McDonalds." A child can also learn a great deal about herself by school time, not just whether she likes vegetables or not, but also what her feelings and experiences mean to her. When she feels hurt, discouraged, or angry she has a lot to say. It is during these moments that she wants our sympathy and wants us to listen and hear who this unique individual is and how it feels to have these experiences. Children also want to share the fun and joy just, as adults do.

39. SHARING

Create many opportunities to share what's happening in the classroom or at home. (Avoid repetitive sharing during which children bring toys and talk in a format). Find ways to challenge children while sharing without making them feel they are on the hot seat. Make a list of possible questions. Have team sharing. Vary the format and strengthen the abilities of the interviewer and interviewee. (See the listening chapter.) Use sharing as a way for children to interact with their academic work as often as possible.

COMMUNICATING WHO WE ARE

We all want to be known and valued for who we are. We want to know that our presence and our lives matter. Interacting responsively and intelligently with children will help them use this marvelous tool of language to connect the dots of their experience to paint a self portrait. A child can come to see herself as a wondrously complex and intelligent being flowing like water through thousands of encounters, problems, and experiences, learning and growing through each. She can see her own magnificence and grow to be an adult full of self-understanding and self-esteem.

---

40. INTERVIEW PROCESS

(For adults or children.) Interview another person. Your interests should determine the interviewee. Try various interview techniques. Create projects in which children can do several different forms of interviewing.

1. *Ask open-ended questions like, "When you get up in the morning, what is the first thing you think about?" Or "When you were a child, what did you dream about doing in your lifetime?" Or "Tell me about yourself?"*

2. *Make a list of questions based in why you are interested in that other person. They can be the who, why, where, when, and how of journalism. The questions can be more limited, such as "How did you make that cabinet reproduction of Quaker furniture?"*

3. *You can use a normal conversational format in which you respond only to elicit more information, such as, "That is interesting: tell me more about it." You may want to limit the time or the parameters of the interview.*

Parents and schools often participate in the atrophy of children's capacity to communicate about themselves. Children who sit passively doing work sheets in the school or watching television each day are not having the rich opportunities to interact with, stimulate, and strengthen their capacity to communicate. Just as learning to talk was a marriage of personal needs and cultural demands, academic learning becomes more and more fascinating when tied to personal processes. When children constantly share, they create space for more information to flow in so that they can share more. Experiences are complex. Sharing them demands subtlety. As children learn to share this complexity more accurately, it will show in sophisticated understanding of academic subjects.

Train yourself in communication. Good communicators teach good communication. Sharing is what we do naturally. A classroom or family sharing format simply acknowledges what goes on between people. In formalized sharing situations, we help children expand their ability to communicate who they are. This satisfies each child's need to be known, seen, and understood. Try this Interview Process (No. 40, page 75) in conjunction with sharing. It will help adults or children learn to know and understand others.

Learning to interview well involves learning to pull back from our own desire to be center stage and make the other person the star. Some people/children do this naturally but many do not.

(INTER) VIEWING OURSELVES

Art is often a child's first language of self-expression. Art makes real the feelings and thoughts that they are having long before they have verbal and written fluency. The need to express and understand themselves and their world is very powerful. (This need can also be served by music and drama.) Art often gives very young children a way to make visually real their desire to relate to and control the world as well as their personal sense of completeness and wholeness. They can do this long before they can talk about it or even understand what they are attempting.

41. SELF PORTRAITS

Have a child/adult draw a picture about him/herself. Then have him/her explain the picture's meaning. Ask questions about the explanation and picture, questions which draw the child out. Respect the child's fears and anxieties about judgement. Mirror what she says about the picture. Perhaps the child will want to draw other pictures about herself. Continue this process: expand the questions and the interactions. It is a way to develop a positive relationship with a child's self-image.

In preschool and kindergarten, I often find children doing art whenever they have the opportunity. Nearly all images that children create are personally meaningful. The very young often draw images of themselves and people in their lives. Children may also draw dinosaurs or monsters or plants and animals. Allowing a child to talk about what they are saying in the pictures further validates their desire to communicate about themselves. It lets them know that this connection with a sense of themselves is good and meaningful to the adults and the world around them.

The value of self portraits does not stop as children become more verbal and can be useful even for high school students. I often see high school students who struggle in most subjects, but who are totally dedicated to their drawing and do it whenever they have free time. Self portraits are not limited to physical images of a person but can be portraits of anything having to do with his or her life. They can consist of portraits of the child's room, a pet, friends, and a car.

As an on-going process, encouraging a flow between the visual, auditory, and verbal may help adolescents and older children through those painful or out-of-control periods of life. If their own creative skills have been nurtured throughout their growth, they will be more than a passive audience to the self-expression of others. They will be able to express themselves through drawings, written stories, or oral self portraits. Self portraits then become a way of coming to grips with a changing life. Creative self-expression is a principle way to extend self-knowledge into the world. It is a safe way of self-revelation and connection with the world at a time when their emerging identities are breaking free of their families and of adult control.

WRITING STORIES AND BOOKS

One of the most successful classroom self-expression projects I have seen was in a fifth grade classroom where the students self-published a story book. It had illustrations, text, and a laminated cover, as well as a copyright indications and a cover page. They made up the story and created all of the illustrations. The sense of interacting with the adult world as peer artists and verbal communicators was very powerful.

JOURNALING

Many classrooms are using journals as language skills workbooks. Students write personally meaningful information. Often, teachers write responses. This way, teachers and student have a private and intimate conversation in a classroom of thirty students. Historically women have used journals to support the personal changes that they have gone through as their role in society has changed. When we read back through our journals or diaries we can see the changes and the solutions to problems. This helps us see that we can deal with change and problems. Journals can be used for self-talk, including both lists of possible solutions to problems, decisions about goals, as well as opinions and records of daily experiences. I would like to encourage adults to help children go back through their journals to get a sense of their own processes and progress. Recently I heard Robert Muller, Secretary General of the United Nation, talk. He has kept a journal and enjoys going back to review his life. His act of acknowledging his accomplishments gives him the courage to move forward.

42. JOURNAL

Keep a journal. You can write about a variety of things that are important to you. You may record details of your life or world, just as you would in a diary. You may record goals, dreams, stories - an infinite variety of perspectives on your own life. You may paste in photos, pictures, and related materials such as newspaper articles. Use it as a primary personal resource tool.

43. AUTOBIOGRAPHY

Have a child/adult create an autobiography. The child can write it down, put it in various drawings, or create other ways of communicating an autobiography. He can do it as play, sport, or some sort of outdoor activity. It can be a theatrical piece, a play, a video, or a stand-up routine. Adults need to be flexible, allowing a variety of possible ways that a child can organize her awareness of her life. You can interview on tape or videotape. You can let the child interview you, other members of his family, and other children.

44. ANOTHER AUTOBIOGRAPHY PROJECT

Create a video or photo biography of children. Interview them on video; or document their favorite food, toy, games, their friends, clothes they like to wear, their favorite entertainment, and their fantasies. Create a sense of a whole life. Then do this from time to time. Utilize it as a record of children and various things they have accomplished. Both of you can review the video/written biography to see how much growth and accomplishment has occurred.

Autobiographies are a more structured telling of our story. The format can vary, but we are front and center. Autobiographies are helpful in chronicling different stages in a person's life. Remember we adults do not get to vote on a child's being. We may help with technical aspects of the creation of a project. But we need refrain from critiquing the content, what sort of person the child is, and how the child feels about herself. Support the positive statements and allow the child to voice and let go of the difficulties and pains.

I interviewed my six-year-old grandson, Nikki, about his life. I asked him how it felt to be born — he said, "good." — and how was it when he was an infant, "fine." He thought he was probably "cute" when he was little: he's seen photos. He liked to nurse and have his diapers changed, he was sure. Is this really what he felt? Or does that matter? It was a good day for Nikki and I as we walked along the park and I interviewed him. We stopped when he was tired of the game. I asked him if he liked being interviewed. He did. I asked him how he felt about himself right now. He said, "good." This was a very simple conversation but it was as important as any conversation.

Classroom teachers can make a physical outline portrait of a child at the beginning and end of the school year. This way the child can see how much he has grown over the year.

You can use this Biography(Nos. 43 and 44, page 79) project in conjunction with goal setting. This project helps to counter feelings of being overwhelmed by problems, because we can see how naturally we have solved other problems in the past. It also helps to counter the tendency to focus upon our shortcomings rather than our strengths.

Have children write and draw their life stories frequently. Allow these stories to be entirely their choice. You can talk about the relationship between fiction and accurate recording of events in one's life. They can fictionalize their lives and create books. They can make up adventures in them. Perhaps they can create a fantasy about when they will become a teenager. This exercise is excellent for developing their writing skills, and their capacity to perceive and understand themselves.

ORAL HISTORIES

Oral histories can empower a group, such as a family. Children get to know members of the family better. See their accomplishments, their struggles, their values, and the basic problems and issues that the family has had to deal with, perhaps generation after generation. Virginia Satir's family reconstructions permit much healing between parents and children when children can see why the parents made the decisions that they did. Let children be in charge of this oral history process: they will find the information and it will make sense to them. Understanding why and how we make decisions is a very important part of maturing.

45. CREATING AN ORAL HISTORY

Children can write or carry a recording tape machine or camcorder. They interview family members, people in the community who know their family, and family friends. You can make an extensive family oral history taken over a period of time, as a class assignment or a family project. Ask all sorts of detailed questions about who, when, where, how, why. Fit the pieces together generation by generation, or period by period in your own family.

AUTONOMY AND CHILDHOOD

Young children don't have a great sense of their separateness from the adults in their lives. Autobiographical and Journal (pages 78, 79) work help to develop this sense of their separate actions, desires and thoughts. Personal growth for children is the establishment of a separate identity. Often this involves rebellion against adults, because in rebellion children clearly see that they are different (basically opposite!) from adults. Being able to stand back and see how they are unique and perceive their emerging identities through Autobiographical projects will help to lessen the rebellion. A gradual series of assertions of identity will help adolescents avoid many negative repercussions, such as drinking and driving, drugs, promiscuity, and self-destructive behavior that can come with rebellion.

VERBAL COMMUNICATION: INTENTION

When we say or ask something of someone and get a confusing or negative response, we tend to be discouraged or even angry. When we hear a request, we not only hear the words but the feelings and thoughts behind the words. People respond to the intention behind our communications as well as the words we say. When the intention and the words are aligned, then the communication is effective. People respond to what we say. They are less likely to be confused or resistant. We are effective: we get action. When our deeper intentions are in conflict with what we are saying, we are often not effective. We get responses very different from those we envisioned.

46. TELEPHONE

Sit in a circle. One person starts whispering a message in the ear of the person next to her. Then it goes around the circle with each person whispering in the ear of the person next to him or her. See if the message, the intention behind it, and even the emotional tone of voice are the same when it gets back to the originator.

Children love to play telephone. One can see the communication differences between boys and girls as early as the third grade. When children learn that conscious expression of intention often gets others to hear and respond to their communication, they can learn assertiveness at a early point in their lives.

47. OBSERVING
LEVELS OF COMMUNICATION

Observe communication. Make a mental note of what you think is not being said as well as what is being said. Notice the different ways people say things to one another. Notice how people go about getting attention, creating and maintaining relationships, and getting needs met. You can do this with children as well. You can have them observe what happens on the playground or outside. Then have them compare notes, becoming young sociologists and anthropologists. They can notice differences/similarities in communication affected by power, attitudes, culture groups, male-female dynamics, and age.

We have learned many coping strategies in order to participate in life. John Bradshaw and other authors who study codependency acknowledge this variety in the various roles that people play in families. Many of these coping strategies are not effective. That is, they create more conflict than success as individuals make their way through life. Learning to observe the multilevel nature of communication, the varying intentions within even the most innocent conversation, is the first step toward learning effective interaction.

48. BEING AWARE OF THE INTENTION BEHIND COMMUNICATION

Observe people communicating. Listen actively and carefully. Can you determine that person's actual intent? Can you guess what he or she is saying from various other qualities of the communication, such as body language, or the mood? What are you experiencing in your body or in your feelings? Use this as a game or listening process with others. Then give them feedback about what you are guessing. See if you have been accurate. See where you have been mistaken.

49. DIFFERENT KINDS OF TALKING

Play this game. Find a statement or conversation - any communication. Now play with it. See how many different ways you can say the same things? Talk about how the meanings change when the worlds are spoken differently. You can make lists on a board or piece of paper. Give players on different teams points for each different way of saying something. Points for all of the different interpretations of what is said.

COMMUNICATING "I" ISSUES.

To communicate your own point of view simply, use "I" statements. I was trained academically to use "you" statements. They are very hard to get away from in writing and in verbal communication. They are the normal frame of enmeshment in our society. By using "you" statements, we are identifying with a prevalent "right" point of view held by some ultimate authority. So we parents say to our children, "You should be cleaning your room," rather than, "I feel very uncomfortable when the house is messy, and I would appreciate if if you would help me." "I" statements make me responsible for my life, feelings, and world. They are a powerful way for me to be myself. At first it is very scary to use "I" statements because most of society doesn't use them. In journalism, nonfiction writing, and public address the "you" form is the standard. As we learn to frame our feelings and thoughts with "I," we find we have less conflict with others and feel more freedom in talking about ourselves

In terms of self-esteem, it is more important for children to learn to talk about themselves, effectively and with conviction, than to talk about presidents or science. Information communicated through education is a large collection of fragments. These fragments only come together and make sense within the context of each individual child. When placed within a framework of a strong positive sense of self, the child can utilize the information and the skills she learns to express her point of view. However, if she has a weak or poor sense of who she is, then she feels somehow obligated to all the values, viewpoints, information, and skills of other people. In a sense, she is wandering through life without a compass— a compass to measure the way things are with regard to who she is. She also has far less reason, as her education goes on, to acquire more information and more skills. She has been gathering all of this information but its use to her is unknown. Pretty soon the load gets heavy and seems useless. She may say to herself, "What can one more fact about math or American history have to do with whether my friends like me or not?"

50. "I FEEL" EXERCISE

Have a discussion using "I" words, a self-referential approach. Take full responsibility for everything you believe, feel, notice, and see. (Use "I" language in the various exercises in this book.)

51. "I FEEL" OBSERVATION

When making "I" statements, notice how it feels to be in charge of everything going on in your mind and your feelings. Try utilizing the "I" form in communication consistently over a period of time. Notice how different it is from general "you" focused conversation. See what you notice about how the world opperates in terms of communication. See if you become aware of the ways your talking functions.

OBJECTIVITY

We have all been trained in depersonalized learning and experience. The objective point of view theory is no longer held in advanced work in physics and astronomy. Stephen Hawking tells us in "A Brief History of Time," that in observing we affect what is being observed. (1.) Advanced science is now recognizing its subjectivity. How much more subjective must be thinking in history or social sciences. Yet the world of the classroom and university have yet to catch up with modern physics of the last 90 years.

"I" STATEMENTS AND CONFLICT RESOLUTION

Granted, we won't start our science lesson tomorrow with the statement, "I feel the earth is round." However, we can learn to talk about what we feel. Often teachers are expected to be referees, choosing between right and wrong in a conflict. By changing the dynamic of conversation to one focused upon feelings, children can learn to resolve their own disputes. They can learn to lay out the different feelings, miscommunications, and assumptions that caused the initial misunderstanding, then they can work on the problems that lie beneath the conflict.

52. CONFLICT RESOLUTION PROCESS

Bring the conflicting parties together. An uninvolved group will serve as the facilitator. (Request a resolution to the conflict or a specific outcome that is satisfactory to each party.) Encourage the conflicting parties to use "I" statements as much as possible. Have each tell her/his side of the conflict. The facilitators act as mirrors. The facilitators actively listen and use their intuition and empathy to ask questions or have the conflicting parties restate things, clarify, or expand. The purpose is to have the conflicting parties find their own solution to the problem. This can be used for both adults and children. (At the conclusion the conflicting parties can make a verbal or written agreement that formally acknowledges the outcome.)

In this process, facilitators must learn to refrain from fixing the conflict, deciding who is right or wrong, or showing the conflicting parties where the solution lies. They learn to draw the disputants out. To find out what each one is feeling and experiencing. In becoming a great conflict resolution facilitator, we develop our listening power into a finely tuned instrument. When people have been truly heard and know that someone is aware of their problem, they can let go of the sense of conflict or confrontation. Often, we hold onto our point of view, gripe, or sense of injustice because we do not feel that we are being understood. We feel that our existence is being ignored. We feel that others are riding roughshod over our needs, feelings, and beliefs when we have disagreements with others. Often, conflicts involve two or more people who feel ignored and misunderstood. When they're understood, the solutions are quite simple and quite acceptable to both parties. Conflict Resolution between children, using children as facilitators, can be an active part of school playground and classroom procedures.

53. SAME AND DIFFERENT

Have children/adults share. How are they the same? How are they different from others? This is very helpful for male/female issues and problems, as well as multi-ethnic/racial classrooms. The sharing should not be judgemental, that is sameness and differences are the way things are on planet Earth. You may take this exercise to the level of feelings and experiences as the children become skilled at it. It is helpful to have this be an ongoing classroom or parent-child exercise, once a week, or even several times a week. There are many ways of sharing this. One is by listing. Another is by describing in great detail what they know is different and the same. They may write plays or skits, draw, create events or parties, etc. Ensure that each child's contribution is held in the same esteem as all others.

COMMUNICATION IS A GROWTH PROCESS

Many of us have learned to hide ourselves from others, to protect our vulnerable inner feelings. Changing withdrawal patterns takes time. Hiding out from other people is common, so revealing one's self, telling the world who we are, may take a lot of courage and practice. With practice, children can become very good at differentiating their feelings from those of adults and other children. By using "I" statements, they begin to see their thoughts, beliefs and goals.

In our attempts to be objective, to present some supposed, educationally correct point of view, we ignore children and teach them to deny their existence. We tend to equate objectivity with fairness. Yet fairness is really about allowing all points of view. We assume that children absorb information because it is objective, though in truth they absorb information because it is personally meaningful.

The belief that there is only one way of seeing things (even an so-called "objective" one) automatically creates conflicts with every other viewpoint. If we acknowledge that each person has a different viewpoint and, if we allow some time each day for self-expression, we can reassure children that their unique process of learning won't be buried. They won't be asked to ignore their own existence in the process of acquiring information. They won't come to believe there is a conflict between their need to express themselves and society's need that they learn a certain body of subject matter.

DIFFERENT KINDS OF "LEARNERS"

There are visual, spatial, auditory, and kinesthetic learners. It is time to realize that every learning process is unique and specific to that individual child. Although it looks like every child learned how to walk and talk the same way, any parent will tell you about the different timing and approaches of different siblings.

DISEMPOWERING COMMUNICATION

Effective communication happens between equals: disempowering communication happens with a perception of huge power or knowledge gaps. Equality means that we all have differences in experiences and expertise. I am not a lawyer or a doctor but that gives them no advantage over me. Any child I meet is whole and complete. Our experiences and our lives are the equal to anyone's. That is why it is important to validate what children do know and refrain as much as possible from correcting it with so-called superior adult learning. Children can learn to correct themselves when it becomes necessary. We adults also must recognize that much adult learning is only opinion; we do not possess ultimate objective wisdom.

54. OBSERVING POWER DIFFERENCES IN COMMUNICATION

Observe communication between people in your life. Notice the signs or means by which one person indicates that he or she thinks he/she is more important, powerful, or worthy than another person. Notice gestures and ways of stating one's ideas. Notice command language, "do this" type statements. Notice the implications beneath power communications. Particularly notice implications of coercion. The "do this or else" type of statement. Notice these communications in association with race, sex, job, age, and socio-economic status.

Strategies to teach will only be partially effective as long as conditions within the classroom or family suggest inequality. We need to recognize that in communication there are more factors acting toward suppressing and inhibiting communication than there are factors toward freeing it, empowering it, or making it effective. By initially identifying power issues, we can create frameworks for communication that allow us to get beyond them. Other factors inhibiting communication are fear, shame, cultural prohibitions, a sense of injustice, and anger.

CHINESE PUZZLES

We are like a Chinese puzzle. Each layer that we inspect leads to another layer, each intricate and fascinating. But it is impossible to look at these layers without others becoming conscious of the fact that we are looking. To the degree that we are able to share these layers with others, we are able to move on to the layers beneath and so forth. In staying superficial in our relationships with others, we remain superficial in our relationship with ourselves. It is the nature of awareness. It is a mutual process. We find our understanding reflected in our interaction with other people. When we see our self-knowledge reflected, in how they respond to us, it adds strength to and confirms our understanding. If we feel good about ourselves, we see that others feel good about us too. We also notice that they come to feel good about themselves, even when they are not actively engaged in strengthening their own self-esteem.

Subtlety of understanding of oneself gained from examining these layers gives one great mastery over life. It creates the Shakespeares and Rembrandts of history. Our reactions no longer surprise us; we begin to stop reacting in mindless ways. We respond to the world from deeper places within, places of greater wisdom and understanding. The deeper one goes, the richer the journey of life. Why deprive children of this? They cannot understand Shakespeare when their capacity to understand their own feelings and experiences is intentionally or unintentionally kept limited and restricted for fear that it might unloose a Pandora's box. We may block children's communication because we fear our own feelings. By preventing others from knowing of their feelings we also are incapable of knowing about our own.

OPENING COMMUNICATION

When I paint a picture, I feel around in my mind for a mood and then let that mood lead me. If I tell you about my process, perhaps you will tell me the ways you are intuitive. Perhaps it will be your intuitive solution to a computer program. Then we both are encouraged to continue using our intuition. I talk to you about my intuition because I sense that it is safe. We can only share at a mutual comfort level. In order to open communication, we need to work in very structured ways. Here's a central process for opening communication, called "The Insight Process." Use it in every conceivable way and your communication with others will continuously improve.

55. THE INSIGHT PROCESS

Group size may vary, works for families as well.

1 .*Each person talks until finished. For larger groups, use a pack of cards and distribute them. The participants take their turn according to their number.*

2. *No one interrupts. (Teachers and parents may need to do the process a few times before including children, so that they allow children to be full participants.)*

3. *Confidentiality. What is said in the process is not repeated elsewhere. It is a "safe" space. Participant's integrity and privacy is respected. If this is maintained, openness can exist.*

4. *No insults, put-downs, name calling, or abuse of others.*

5. *Tell it as you see it. Take full responsibility for what you say. As much as possible, use "I" statements. (Pay attention to individual's efforts toward projection of responsibility on others.)*

6. *Work toward curtailing the listing of grievances or blame. Work toward bringing the talk back to what the individual has to communicate about her or himself.*

Process: Schedule this process regularly and in a comfortable and safe environment. For families and classes, once a week is good. You can schedule extra sessions when problems or issues arise. The person setting it up will write down or tell the group the ground rules. You may, at that point, establish the parameters — what you want to talk about. Optimally each person talks until finished. You may need to limit time for each talker (with a timer). When you start this process, it may take a while before the rules are appreciated. Enthusiasm may lead participants to want to interrupt. With practice, any group can do it. Continue until everyone who wants to talk has talked. As it becomes safer, everyone will begin to participate.

The Insight Process has innumerable uses for solving problems and opening up communication to a more democratic forum. When first used, it may present some difficulties, because most participants will experience freedom that they have rarely had: the lid is lifted off. Without the usual repressive forms of communication, the sense of access is very exciting. I have found that children of all grade levels are enthusiastic and excited. But they also can get carried away. Many early sessions may need to be dedicated to exploring the implications of such available communication, how it feels for other participants when you say things that might harm others. How it feels to be interrupted. How it feels when there are hisses, cheers, or groans. How it feels when certain groups of participants try to get together and gang up on other individuals or groups.

When you start using the Insight Process, you will begin to identify some of the problems in communication that take place regularly. If you are attentive, you will work through chronic communication problems and in time they will disappear. This is why it is important to observe the guidelines, especially to refrain from put-downs, for they tend to create conflict and prevent all participants from paying attention to feeling. As participants become accustomed to the process and the rules, they will willingly observe rules which they see serve to create a sense of freedom and access to communication.

This process retrains us with regard to old habits of power, control, and domination. In ordinary conversation one person may try to only communicate certain things or prevent others from communicating things that he/she does not want to hear. If we trust the Insight forum, this habit will become as clear to the controller as it is to those controlled. Empowerment is the underlying goal of the Insight Process for self-esteem work. When a participant knows her contribution is valuable, she knows she is valuable.

THE INSIGHT PROCESS IN SPECIAL EDUCATION

Creating a safe environment is key to the success of this process. In special education classes that use a similar process, it is very important that what is said in the room not leave that room. Violating this trust is violating another person's and the group's integrity and privacy. With special needs students, the process is closely monitored to ensure that even subtle put-downs or complaints against another person are dealt with verbally immediately. If a child hit another on the playground, each person's side of the story is communicated. The circle hears how it felt on both sides. The children may or may not decide to settle it there. However, in special education situations, ground rules may dictate that these matters be settled before the circle is ended. General use can leave problems unresolved, acknowledging that sometimes solutions evolve.

Repetitive use of such a process takes the children toward responsibility for behavior as they get to hear the repercussions from the mouth's of others who are affected. They are neither obliged or immediately allowed to justify or defend themselves. The time lapse between hearing and responding may give them time to incorporate the other's experience into their approach to the issue. Often with fights and conflict, the anger and hurt begins to dissipate and ultimately they are able to forgive and become friends. When a teacher or parent is an arbiter and dispenser of justice often, the resentments are simply maintained and children find ways of getting even away from the eyes of authority. By the time children reach junior high and high school, they have had so many years of adults dispensing so-called justice that all sorts of resentments and group hostilities have built up. This leads to various behaviors, such as gangs and violence in and out of the schools.

PROBLEM-SOLVING

The Insight Process can be used regularly to solve classroom or family problems or to deal with goals. The Insight Process is good preparation for the Conflict Resolution Exercise (page 85) in dealing with fights, gang behavior, and other disruptive conflicts. The problem or goal is stated and then each person is allowed, in safety, to talk about it until he or he has had his say. The regularity of the process aids long-term classroom, family, and personal goals. If you decide to solve a problem by using the Insight Process, but don't do the process again while the solution is being worked out, conflicts and misunderstandings inherent in other ways of communicating may come up and sabotage solutions. The Insight Process isn't magic. It simply gives room for different points of observation or interaction in communication.

ATTACK/DEFENSE

Being aware of attack/defense communication habits will be helpful in working with open communication. Sometimes we attack — telling another person they've done wrong or that they have character defects. The other person may defend themselves against our attack. Or we may defend ourselves, constantly fearing an attack. After a while our minds automatically move into attack/defense communication strategies. Sometimes defenses obsess us in specific situations or around particular people or in settings in which we feel fearful, unsure, and anxious. The attack/defense form of communication is very painful, and brings most forms of open communication to a halt. Children become masters of this form quite quickly. For them it is just another way that adults talk to one another. In using the Insight Process, participants can start an attack/defense sequence and it can run on, totally monopolizing the process and violating the guidelines. Participants will forego taking turns, making "I" statements, and loose track of what the process has accomplished. In a sense a war has started. This observation exercise helps sensitize us to attack/defense communications.

56. OBSERVE ATTACK/DEFENSE

Observe attack and defense communications around you. See if you can tell when attack stops and defenses begin. See if you can understand what is being defended. See if you can understand what is being attacked. Notice your feelings as you observe others utilizing attack or defense strategies in communication. Are they trying to establish power, justice, or redress grievances? How successful are they in accomplishing what seems to be the underlying reason for this communication? Are there other ways they could have communicated this more effectively?

COMMUNICATION AND DENIAL

It is important to have a forum for children and/or adults to talk about their feelings. It is important to let them learn to deal with their own issues and problems rather than solving problems for them. This support takes time and ongoing communication. If we distract or turn conversation to our personal fears or thoughts, we tell them they don't matter. Constantly turning attention away from the issues within a family or within a classroom is a process of denial. We deny things because they are too difficult, too painful, because we fear them, or because we think they take too much time and are unimportant. When we deny, we teach children to deny. When an adolescent is asked why she became pregnant or why he was driving drunk and they say they don't know, self-denial may be the root. They no longer have contact with suppressed feelings and thoughts motivating their behavior.

By substituting lessons about the world for knowledge and understanding of what's inside and the insights about personal experiences, we are giving children a substitute life and aiding in the processes of denial. This substitute life, if it is all that is validated, will slowly act to distract from or deaden self-understanding. It is not surprising that street life has such a real life, real rewards appeal.

MALE VERSUS FEMALE ISSUES

One of the major self-esteem problems among children from the fourth or fifth grade onward has been the male-female relationship. Psychologists suggest that this sex role differentiation is natural. Yet hostility and tendency to project all of one's problems onto the other sex is not. By the time children reach high school, the hostility coupled with lack of training in communication skills creates tension between boys and girls. Symptoms of conflict among teenage couples manifest in physical abuse, teen pregnancies, and date rape. Communication training from kindergarten onward could help to avoid so many of the issues between men and women. If we don't talk to each other, how are we to know what is going on with each other? If we don't talk openly, we must rely on rumor, stereotypes, and on all of the unexpressed and covert messages we hear in the adult world. If we only talk around sanctioned text books and worksheets instead of around the reality of each other's lives, we will get the stilted and indirect forms of communication we see in the schools today. This communication amounts to posturing around sex roles and the covering up of deep feelings of inadequacy, and talking around pain and fear of rejection.

I met Brent in a high school art class that I taught. He was a very attractive high school senior, a football star, and a excellent student. While at a weekend get-away senior party he got drunk and fell from a roof, and died. Brent seemed to have it all, be riding at the top of the world. Yet he died while acting out the dangerous nature of his bravado. Brent identified masculinity with high performance which led him to numb himself with alcohol so he could hide his fears and feelings. Included in these were rational fears for his own safety. In his pursuit of being admired by his classmates, he was willing to sacrifice intimacy with his own feelings and vulnerablity. The loss of Brent is a tragedy for his family and his society, as is the loss of any child.

Jeanie had her first child when she was 18. It was her way of having someone to love and to love her. Her mother had gone through various losses while Jeanie was growing and had neglected paying attention to her. Her mother was passing on her personal lack of self-esteem to her daughter having not dealt with all of her own suffering and personal issues. This mother denied or ran from her sense of inadequacy and failure. Because Jeanie had her child out of a sense of inadequacy, she was not well prepared for the sort of care and nurturing required. Furthermore, she was a teenager and would still have to find a way to support herself and her child. Jeanie and her mother started to work on these issues and managed to terminate the cycle. They were supported in this process by other caring adults. Today many self-help groups have been created as support networks to help individuals work through deeply rooted self-esteem problems.

57. THE INSIGHT PROCESS
IN DEALING WITH SEX ROLES

(For K-12) Discuss sex roles. Topic questions:

1. What is the difference between boys and girls? 2. How are boys and girls alike? 3. Why do boys and girls (men and women) have so many problems between them? 4. When you grow up, how do you want males and females to relate to one another? 5. How do your parents or other adults in your life relate to each other differently as males and females?

(For high school ages.) 6. How do you feel about sexual issues such as rape, pregnancy, sexual harrassment, birth control, and sexually transmitted diseases? 7. What part do you think sex plays in a healthy life? 8. Other issues?

Tolerant and patient parents and teachers can allow children's fears about their sex role identity to come out without labeling these fears bad or wrong. When the fears of being different, weird, or unacceptable come out, children see how common such fears are and that they are OK. Tolerance produces the Safe Space necessary to release fears and find a healthy acceptance of one's identity. In the Insight Process, we practice tolerance for different points of view or thoughts. We can learn respect and compassion so that we don't violate one another's integrity or point of view. If allowed to see their own lack of tolerance or respect, instead of being corrected or shamed for it, they won't feel the need to defend it. They won't become entrenched. They won't take it up as a badge of identity, as the contemporary skinheads have. Talking about tolerance allows people to be aware of intolerance.

CREATING A SAFE SPACE

Many of the topics, such as "how boys and girls are different or the same," can be initially dealt with obliquely or intellectually in more academic Insight discussions. In junior high and high school sex education classes the amount of distancing through denial and disparagement is great. Even in very early grades, the amount of emotional heat or intensity around topics of gender role and sex is great. There is discomfort, shame, embarrassment, and often emotional pain due to experiences of sexual violation. Thus for Insight discussions to be ultimately successful in assisting children and adolescents in taking charge of their lives and their identities, the environment in which it is discussed and learned needs to be safe. Creating a Safe Space may be one of the most difficult processes a teacher or adult undertakes.

58. EXPERIENCE A SAFE SPACE

Sit quietly, eyes closed. Imagine an experience in which whatever you said or felt was considered OK. Imagine other people being with you in that experience; see their loving and compassionate faces, see them smile lovingly, and see them listen to you. Feel yourself being supported by these people. See that whatever you say or feel is just fine with those people. See that you are deeply understood and acknowledged and respected by these people.

In a Safe Space each child's individual identity is respected and acknowledged. No child is disparaged or made to feel inadequate. In communicating about sex role identity we often need to have achieved great integrity and commitment to the Insight Process to go beyond fear and shame. These are initial guidelines for a safe space. The reasons for these guidelines should be understood and agreed upon by all participants.

59. SAFE SPACE

Use the Insight process: Talk about what would be a safe space. What about relationships with others feels unsafe? Why have integrity in dealing with others? Why tell the truth? What does confidentiality mean? Can you keep a secret? Do you believe others can keep secrets? What affects your trust of others? What sort of information would you fear having others know? What sort of knowledge of you would be least frightening if others knew it? What does it mean to acknowledge another person? How does it feel to know that you can talk about yourself and that others will choose not to make comments or judgments against you? In what regard should others affect what you do, how you feel, and what you think? What do you feel should be the limits to the influence of others upon you and your life?

Make a Safe Space Contract for each participant to sign in which you agree to keep all of the listed conditions of your safe space. Decide on what will happen for people who do not keep the contract.

SAFE SPACE AND PERSONAL REVELATION

To further move learning to the personal, children may want to talk about their feelings about themselves and about others. In the context of a Safe Space, this means that the guidelines insist that whatever is communicated within the space cannot be used outside of the space. That is, children cannot use what they learn about other children to take advantage of that other child, to make disparaging comments, or to abuse either emotionally or physically. Children can't go into the playground and call other children names based on what they learned in an Insight circle. This level of restraint demands great discipline and commitment to others. Children may need to do the process for months and even years before they will be willing to reveal much about themselves in the face of the possibility of betrayal.

If the Process of Insight were to move to very personal comments, then it must be monitored closely and violations of the integrity of the process taken seriously. Those who couldn't maintain integrity and confidentiality could be denied access to the process. When this sort of process is used in Special Education classroom with children who have behavioral issues, the parents are closely involved. Teachers may need to include only children whose parents are willing to understand the nature of the process and support it. Parents may object to any Insight or Safe Space work. Their needs and feelings also must be honored. In time some of these parents may find the positive results so enticing that they may want their children to have them as well. Safe Space work is more powerful and more effective as a self-esteem tool as we learn the freedom to express ourselves fully. Permitting Safe Space processes to evolve may take time because of deep societal prejudices against disclosure.

60. AN EMPATHY PROCESS IN SEX ROLE UNDERSTANDING

Close your eyes and become quiet. Imagine yourself being born a different sex (race, ethnic group). Imagine how you would dress and take care of your body. Imagine what you would do, what kind of play, what kinds of work. Imagine what your feelings would be like; what would be important and unimportant? Imagine the sorts of friends you would have and the kind of relationships you would have with your friends when you were the opposite sex (race, ethnic group). Now imagine what it is like to be one of your friends who is not the same sex (race, ethnic group). See that friend in your mind's eye. Imagine how it feels to be that person, to dress like that person, to do the sort of work and/or play that person does. Imagine solving the problems that your friend must solve. Imagine feeling the sort of feelings your friend of the opposite sex (race, ethnic group) feels.

EMPATHY PROCESSES

Various other processes can help prepare participants for circle discussions. When there are boy-versus-girl conflicts or conflicts over race, appearance, status, age, etc., try the above. It can be done repeatedly to help develop the capacity in children and adults to empathize with each other's lives and life problems.

WHY ADULTS FEAR
THAT CHILDREN WILL REVEAL THEMSELVES

There is a part of each of us which is highly threatened by any change, and particularly by change that would benefit our sense of well-being and self-esteem. It may seem strange that we each have this confusion between our deep sense of goodness and fearful everyday thoughts. Yet this confusion can be expressed self-destructively. That is, we may try to undermine our or another person's efforts toward improving self-esteem. Most would not argue that every child should have positive self-esteem. Yet in disparaging arguments against self-esteem projects resides outright fear of anything which deals with what is inside each of us. Ironically, a person who is not firmly centered in a sense of well-being and feels anxious and insecure, child or adult, can lash out at those who wish to help him as well as those who intend harm. He resists because he fears the intrusion of others and feels that his vulnerable feelings might be exposed and ridiculed. In time the positive results of self-esteem programs will convince enough people to give the work a chance.

Adults may fear that even the slightest personal revelation might occur when their children are involved in self-esteem work. They may fear such revelation would not reflect the truth. Parents may be concerned that their children are being involved in processes over which the parents do not have control. These concerns are understandable. Yet the usefulness or benefits of interacting in a Safe Space cannot be ignored. These are powerful processes for unraveling deep conflicts between people and bringing understanding and compassion. To allay such concerns, adults can be aware of what is going on and informed at each step of the process without actually violating the confidentiality of children's communication. Often parental involvement is the basis for Safe Space circle work in Special Education classes.

It is important for schools to involve parents as much as possible in any self-esteem program in the school. Parents can also benefit personally from such work. Many adults have been doing self-help work through books and groups. In the schools, the small "target issue" groups who oppose such interaction can be dealt with by having their children placed in special circumstances when this work is done. That way the majority of children will not be held ignorant for the sake of a minority.

DRAMA

Drama is the premier self-esteem tool. It allows infinite variety of experiential levels of self-learning. This self-learning is low cost and can be done anywhere. All it takes is time and commitment. When we learn from experience we learn on many levels. We learn about all of the senses, interactions, about our own creative potential and that of others, about the intelligence of many people, and of the many abilities that allow the re-creation of even one role, let alone the many roles in a script or play.

From a very early age, children participate in communication which allows them to gain a perspective upon their own lives. They play act. By the time they start talking, they have played for hours in various roles with their toys or other children. Each child may take a role, or one child may take many roles. In play acting, they get to try out all sorts of possibilities which are not necessarily available in their interaction with their ordinary social world. A child can be the parent or the brother instead of the sister. Children can be the beautiful ballerina or the superhero. They can try out various ways of talking and carrying their bodies and even of dressing. They can create paraphernalia to make roles and settings more vivid and fill out the roles more thoroughly. They can do it in the privacy of their own imagination, where they are safe from the intrusion of unwanted interjection from others. This play acting can allow them to resolve conflicts and confusion about their lives and the people they normally communicate with. It also allows them to imagine their own future and imagine themselves as more powerful and effective than they are in their small bodies.

Adults often feel they must take children away from this safe fantasy world to what we call "reality." Thus we often interject and cause children to question what they are doing. We are fearful that they might get stuck in their fantasy world. I suggest that instead parents and teachers learn to support play acting in assisting children to learn about themselves and their process of interacting with life through drama techniques. Play acting is a way to make the very abstractness of the world about them real. If a child can feel and experience that world, then he can feel that he can affect it. As long as the world is a distant phenomenon filled with images he sees on TV or in books, he feels very separate from it. He can be a father or he can be a mother for a while when play acting. Children can be presidents, doctors, trees, bears, and all sorts of different beings or objects. The insights he gains from the roles can make the process of learning in school and at home personally meaningful rather than abstract and irrelevant.

61. DRAMA GAME

Divide children into groups. In each group someone takes turns playing. I give points for the roles because children are used to playing games with winners and losers. But often the need to scorekeep can be lost in the energy around playing the game. The categories for scoring are: 1. EMOTION: (1 pt.) a feeling, expression, such as anger, sadness, joy, etc. 2. ROLE: (2 pts.) a generic role such as mother, father, farmer, doctor, etc. 3. Character (3 pts.) a specific personality such as Elvis, King Lear, Rainman, or the current President, Madonna, Juliet, the school principal, etc. Tell the audience groups whether it is a role, emotion, or a character. Then anyone can guess the precise answer to what is being acted out. If someone guesses correctly, then the actor's group gets the points. The categories are graded according to their potential for a higher level of play acting. Although initially children may find characters which are easy to do, they often like the challenge of more difficult characters. Again it may take time for them to work their way toward doing more difficult characterizations and for the more shy members to participate. But in time they usually join in. Younger children, between the ages of 6 and 10, love this game and will have no trouble getting started.

As a starter I use a drama game as a treat (free play) for children from kindergarten through the 7th grade. If used as a game, over time children can learn many subtleties about human behavior and about how they feel about their roles, especially if it is discussed as well as played.

Role playing can be used to assist in understanding all sorts of situations and conflicts. When we play a role, our bodies and our emotions will respond as if it were real. Then we can learn to pay attention to these feelings and body responses to get to know ourselves better. We also may find that we spontaneously have our own responses to this situation. Our body and automatic reactions take over. Role playing allows us to try out many different responses, in situations where we have trouble dealing with the issues. Say, for instance, someone wants you to do something you don't want to do. You're an adolescent and a friend wants you to try out a drug. You can play the role of the person who is trying to entice you. Play the role of someone making a demand, trying to force another person. Play the part of someone who must do something he doesn't want to do. See how it feels to be tempted, to go through fears of being rejected by friends for being different. If you have been unable to be assertive role playing can teach you assertiveness.

62. ROLE PLAYING

Each person acts out a role in a situation. Set up the situation. It could be anything, ordinary daily events such as shopping, or conflicted situations such as people fighting or someone trying to get you to do something you don't want to do. Assign the roles. Role play. Do it again with a new cast of players. You can vary the roles even in a two person role playing situation, endlessly. Talk about what people feel each time you do it. Work toward understanding your role and the role that others are play.

Use role playing to understand things going on between people. Use it whenever you have problems to be solved. School roles you can play are — macho stud, vamp, priss, clown; students can learn that role playing is fun and good preparation for creating plays and making visible the dramas and fun of life. Students try out the roles and gain a perspective on social dynamics in their lives.

---

63. CREATE PLAYS BASED IN ROLES

Have children and adolescents create plays and scripts about various types of roles. The stories will evolve of their own if the children are in charge of the scripts. For instance, a script could deal with acceptance, despite an abnormality or difference.

Starting with roles helps to define the work involved in drama. We all try them on from time to time. Think of the class nerd, the football star and jock, and the cheerleader. Physical appearance makes up a possible group of role types — act the parts of the Elephant Man, Edward Scissorhands, a blind, or a deaf person. These role plays give children great insight into the struggle that other people have in gaining compassion and respect. They can learn how people with disabilities learn to be assertive on behalf of their own needs, and thereby learn to assert their own rights and needs. Children can also create roles based on racial or ethnic minorities. In classrooms with minorities, it can be fun to have children of one ethnic background play those from another background, if the children remain sensitive to the other children's feelings.

VOICE DIALOGUE

A valuable technique for adult self-exploration can be utilized in children's dramatic presentations.(2.) Each of us has many different aspects to our personalities. In this technique the different parts of the personality are called "voices." We can all talk from a part of us that is still a child or adolescent. Even if we are very young we may find a part that is very old — a part that wants to control the whole of us, a part that is upset or angry, a part that is sad, and so forth. We use these parts of us all of the time. We use the memories of how we have been at different times of our life, memories of how to act under certain circumstances. These memories remain with us not simply as thoughts but also as energies within our body.

64. VOICE DIALOGUE EXERCISE FOR CHILDREN AND ADOLESCENTS

Work in groups or in a circle. This may be seen as a separate practice or you may focus upon roles developed for a play or for role playing. Have each child become quiet. Have each child locate the feeling or quality of character or thought within himself. Allow that thought, feeling, or character to talk. For instance, have the angry part talk. Talk from the happy voice, the strong voice, the wild or famous voice, the sad voice, the adventurer voice, the star athelete voice, scientist voice, etc. Form pairs. One talks from a voice. The other talks to that voice, asking questions and eliciting information about the voice. What is its name, age, what part does it play in that person, etc. Take turns, then talk about how it went.

Use this to help with plays: it gives additional levels of technique and understanding to the above role work. Voice dialogue allows us to relate to the roles from within, to see how we each have the various roles as potentials within us. Even a handicapped person may find the energy for the star athlete within. A fourth grader might use voice dialogue work in creating a play about early explorers. Have the children find that place within themselves that loves adventure and exploring. Now have the children, one at a time, talk from that place that feels like a pioneer. Ask them to tell you how it feel to roam the world looking for new lands to discover? Ask leading questions to draw the voices out. When that voice has talked about exploring, you may want a voice to talk about wild animals in the wilderness, a hunter perhaps.

USING VIDEO WITH CHILDREN

I have hours of video of my children and grandchildren. Video can be used to empower children. We know it to be a powerful tool in seeing the world about us. It can become a powerful tool in assisting children to see themselves as valuable and important contributors to life. Anything that they see on TV can be part of children's process of learning. School study topics can be documented by children on video by using photos, mock situations, experiments, and plays. Teachers can do a weekly portrait of a student on video as suggested in the autobiography section. Children can interview each other. Children can do mock Phil Donahue or Sally Jessie Rafael programs about topics that they are studying in school. This also makes school work a more dynamic and "fun" process in which children learn more than the dry facts. They learn how they present themselves: they learn how others present themselves and the information they are studying.

65. CREATE A TALK SHOW

Take turns being the host. Put other children on the pannel as experts on some school topic. Each person presents their view of the topic. It could be history, science, math, etc. The audience asks questions.

YOUR OWN THEATER

You can bring all of the above techniques and information together to create a very rich learning situation. Theater is not just an art form it is also a way to learn writing, social sciences, and even science information.

If teachers or parents see this as a great way to teach language and reading skills, drama can be a regular and permanent part of each child's learning. Plays can be created for different goals, and interactions with curriculum during a school year. Children can create plays for history and social science units, and plays about foreign countries for geography.

66. PLAY-MAKING

Rather than writing about their lives in a journal, have children create plays about their world. They can also create theater about their fantasy world and their ideas about who they will be when they grow older. There are endless possibilities. Build on what they learn from the drama game. Each child creates a role. Various groups of children get together and put their different roles together into a simple plot. Plots are straight forward. For example: character 1, 2, 3, and 4 decide to do X. But they can't, because Y occurs and tries to stop them. They must learn Z or do A in order to overcome the obstacle and accomplish their goal. Write down characters and plot outlines. A written script or a picture diagram for a script can be created. Costumes and props can be utilized. The production can be done quickly or take weeks, according to the elaborateness of the play. Start with short plays, really extended role playing. As children gain confidence, they can move toward more involved work.

TALKING AND NOT TALKING

Talking about our feelings is something that most people in our society do not do well. We do not have much practice at it and we don't have much confidence about communicating what is going on within us. We fear, often rightly so, that if we expose these feelings they will not be respected or dealt with in a compassionate and caring manner. To nurture self-esteem we must be vigilant and willing to always treat the expression of other people's feelings in compassionate and loving ways. We must also learn the courage to talk about our own feelings clearly and openly. As we come to feel compassion for the feelings of others, we feel compassion for ourselves.

Our feeling of sadness, pain, suffering, and self-loathing are like clouds over our self-love. We can learn to release the source of these feelings which, generally, are from be in the past. In my life I have had a number of experiences I once considered failures. On one occasion I spent many years and much money toward finding a way to produce a children's feature film. In the end, the money was gone and the film, no matter how wonderful, did not become a reality. I have since learned to see that I was doing the very best I could given what I could understand and foresee at the time. Recognizing this, I can allow myself to use this so-called failure as a stepping stone for learning rather than seeing it as proof of my inadequacy as a person. If I see and communicate about myself as a growing human being, the best "me" that I can be at any time, then I come to love and value myself. As I came to talk more fully about the experiences while working on the film project I came to see old patterns in which I felt helpless in the face of reversals. I had to overcome these patterns and learn to continue regardless of setbacks. When I saw the patterns, then I started releasing them. When I was unable to see the patterns, I was constantly and helplessly recreating them.

I have been fortunate in finding people who are willing to listen and be compassionate toward me. We all can become such resources to others. It is often more important that we simply hear a child than give advise. It is much more valuable if she can learn to solve her own problems. These solutions are the valuable foundation for self-esteem. We cannot rush others in the process of self-knowledge and self-revelation. With an ongoing willingness to develop our sense of self-worth, we can use communication as a powerful tool to tell the world who we are and why we are a valuable and important part of it.

A PLACE TO TALK AND A RIGHT TO TALK

Children need access to many safe opportunities to express their feelings; if not expressed, these feelings will be acted out. When a child acts out unexpressed feelings she experiences being out-of-control. Feeling out-of-control escalates and also affects others in her life. When we feel out-of-control, it is difficult for those around us to feel in control.

Often in families and schools, a sense of control is created by suppressing everything that might be different or potentially upsetting. Suppression can result from endless lists of rules and punishments. Suppression creates a pattern of unexpressed feelings and of acting out those unexpressed feelings. When suppression is endemic, children leave the family and the schools with a deep sense of being out-of-control. This may manifest in all sorts of abuses of themselves and others. They have learned to live out-of-control lives, which in turn affect their own children and those they work and live with. The cycle repeats.

From time to time some of us who have learned to live out-of-control lives stop and find teachers who will help us learn to bring our lives into our own awareness. The sense of relief that I have at having found a way out of my patterns is profound. I have found teachers who helped me become aware of my own inner world of feeling, thoughts, and behavior patterns. Before learning to understand and value myself, I believed that the world was cruel, capricious, and out-of-control and that there was no hope for me. When I became aware of why I do things and how I feel when I do them or are about to do them, I began to experience greater mastery or control over my life.

A life consciously emanating from the integrity of our deepest feelings and selves is a life of powerful contribution to our society and our planet. We learn our feelings and deep inner knowledge by listening to them and sharing what we hear with others who care.

Footnotes:

(1.) Hawking, Stephen W.; *A Brief History of Time,* Bantam Books, New York, 1988.

(2.) Stone, Hal, and Sidra Winkelman; *Embracing Our Selves,* Devorss and Co., Marina Del Rey, 1985.

7. PEACE

67. CHAMPION OF PEACE

Guided eyes closed process for children. Imagine you are
your favorite super hero/heroine (Superman, Wonder
Woman, etc.). Imagine a world threatened by disasters. A
world war is breaking out. People are starving and diseases
are rampant. Volcanoes are erupting. Tidal Waves,
earthquakes, floods, hurricanes, and terrible droughts
strike the Earth. You are going to save the world. What do
you do first? What next? See yourself doing these things.
See what happens. How can you save the earth?

A whole area of education training called "classroom management," has been developed out of the basic belief that we must
put order into uncontrollable elements in human interaction. Yet
the peace and order that we want already exists in each and
every one of us. All we need do is encourage this natural peacefulness to express itself.

We impose discipline, control or order because we believe it
does not exist naturally. If we believe that everybody is potentially
disruptive, out-of-control, and unpeaceful, we will also bring
these qualities to the surface and make them part of the world we
experience. In trying to prevent disruptive behavior, we become
aggressive, anxious, and fearful. Others, who sense it, become aggressive, anxious and fearful in response. When we force things
to be a certain way we oppose the already existing order. This op-
position brings resistance which we then must counter, and this
brings more resistance. We must get a bigger and bigger stick to
impose order from without. We communicate our belief in mis-
behavior by ominously waiting for disaster, and when it comes we
are not surprised. Even in the country schools where I teach,
children are bringing weapons.

Behind a lot of classroom management and adult interaction
with children is a fear that things will get out of hand. Principals are
the trouble shooters and teachers are disciplinarians, believing
they must control children. It is difficult not to get caught up in the

pervasive belief that a greater sense of being out-of-control demands greater control. Yet the more we try to control, the more tense we become. Those who control the situation have a strong sense that if what they are doing is upset or threatened all will shatter. If the compulsion to control becomes pervasive, the tension and stress can become palpable. Children will be anxious and edgy, and small things flare up. In the midst of such a climate, it takes a great deal of faith in human desire for peace to simply relax and trust that all will be well. In letting go of the compulsion to control, we are going against hundreds of years of tradition. Because we all learned that, "The best defense is a good offense."

68. AWARENESS OF EXPECTATIONS OF PEACE

This is a very private exercise. It may be a difficult one to do. See if you can notice people who are anticipating good or peace. See if you can notice people who are anticipating something awful happening. If you can, try anticipating something terrible happening to you. Notice how your body tenses, how our mind reacts. See how the people around you react to these feelings. Now try anticipating only peace in your life, only good will between people, only happy interactions. Anticipate these from the deepest part of your being. See how people around you act when you expect only peace. Clue: If you get in touch with the deep peace within yourself, it's easier to expect only peace.

TRUST AND SURVIVAL

We feel responsible for children and other people. We do not expect children to take care of themselves or provide certain survival needs. No person is an island. The exchange of money for work and services does not terminate the sort of trust we must place in other people's involvement in our survival. People act out of loving compassion and care toward one another, whether they know each other or not. Yet we forget this truth. We forget the cooperative nature of human interactions by expecting children to behave according to society's demands. Then we are surprised when they rebel against such demands. Each person has a choice. When we demand "do it our else," rebellion is the "or else" response. For adults, demands may be made by police forces and employers. Coercion has the quality of creating an institutional setting full of rules and "or else."

Using intervention or intrusion of authority, a controlling person, is quick and efficient. However, long term consequences may not be considered at the time that authority is summoned. Policing rather than gaining cooperation leads participants to relinquish responsibility and commitment. They become disaffected and alienated. It takes time to gain cooperative interaction with others. However, such a commitment of time is worth it; it is the basis for peaceful and responsible behavior, and cooperative relationships where such cooperation is honored, respected, and valued.

MISTRUST OF PEACE

We often mistrust peace because we have been in relationships with people who seemed to want to have peace at any price. These people seem to give up to avoid the anxiety, upset or disruption. Becoming peaceful does not mean that we forget the problems and we deny the pain. We can be honest about what is going on with us and still work toward the goal of peace. Perhaps our present sense of peace is not totally perfected. However, as we decide each time to have peace instead of prolonged anger, upset, or a sense of being out-of-control, we find that we are getting better and better at establishing peace. And peace feels good. Once we get use to having it all the time, we find it hard to believe that we once felt upset and anxious. It becomes harder to believe that we thrive on stress, turmoil, and living on the precipice of life. When we have peace we begin to notice the high cost that conflict and strife have on us and the people around us.

This exercise is my personal peace process in which I usually sort through my feelings to find ones that have to do with specific reactions.

69. A PERSONAL PEACE PROCESS

When you notice that you are not at peace, check out the other feelings that come up, (feelings of hurt, distress, anger, etc.). Spend some time with the feelings specific to this moment. Let yourself have these feelings, to feel rejection, hurt, etc. Maybe you will wish for something to cause it to pass. Have this thought, too. Notice whether you think "What's the point of wanting it to go away it will never go away?" Allow all of the thoughts, anxieties, and fears to come up into your conscious mind. And when they have, let yourself know that you are at peace deep within. It is OK to have these thoughts and at the same time have a part of you be at peace. As you notice this, you may begin to notice that the peace is constant and the thoughts come and go. Practice this often. Peace awareness will grow stronger.

In the process of coming to peace, I may feel that my anxieties, angers, and sadness, sense of injustice, or physical hurt are things that I want to talk to a therapist or counselor about. Or I may want to talk to a family member or friend, or write a letter. As I have learned to come back into an equilibrium with the peacefulness deep within, my confidence grows about being calm while at the same time going about solving the problem or dealing with the issue the gave rise to my anxiety or conflict. In equilibrium, I see the initial emotional turmoil in the perspective of my whole life, my inner journey, and my personal processes. In a sense I carry my "Peace Chair" with me everywhere.

PEACE CHAIR

I often see "time out chairs" in classrooms or homes and think they could be better utilized by making them available to children who want quiet time to feel good about themselves and deal with problems that arise. Instead, they are generally used as punishment. They mark the child as bad and the atmosphere as out-of-control. When tensions arise, children know it. They do not like it any more than adults. Children want peace and harmony as much as adults. They can be given an alternative to punishment in a Peace Chair. Even if it is simply a conceptual alternative, it changes expectations of the household or classroom from ones of order at all costs to ones of peace and harmony. A Peace Chair can be seen as a haven, a place of refuge, and a way to signal a parent or classmates and teacher that things may not be well. Try this exercise for young children and with those up to the 6th or 7th grade.

70. CREATING A SANCTUARY

Create a Peace Chair in your home or classroom for peace/quiet. Allow children to go there according to their own need. Perhaps it can be a corner where they will not be viewed by or communicated to by other children. It can be a very comfortable and nurturing situation. Perhaps you can even allow young children to go there when they are very distressed and crying. They can go there after they are comforted. In creating guidelines to use such an area, we need to understand that this is not for escape, withdrawal, or avoidance of responsibility for something the child might have done. Adults can monitor the chair and utilize it as a way of staying in touch with a child's distress. If used honestly and with the intent to be of assistance, it will be less likely to be misused. For instance the adult can use it to talk to the child about a distressing issue. Time can be set aside to talk, after the child has had time to feel better or get his/her behavior together.

This quiet chair will grant children many benefits. It will help them to acknowledge that their feelings belong to them, and that they have the right to experience their feelings. It will allow them safety and privacy in a setting in which peer or family pressure can be intense. It may begin to help them come to terms with very difficult feelings. Adults need to recognize that children also want to feel in control of their world. They want ways of dealing with what is happening to them, ways that are safe and caring.

As with everything we talk about in this book, coming to peace is a process. At first there may be much demand or little demand for the Peace Chair. You can suggest that a child try it or use it. But don't force them. Let it be their own decision. Otherwise, it is simply another form of punishment and control. Don't give up on the idea, if you can see the underlying advantage of it over other approaches. Return to it, and make this idea of safety in experiencing one's feelings central. If viewed as a goal and a process peace can be an ongoing experience.

PUNISHMENT

In many classrooms and households punishment is used to obtain acceptable behavior. It may be part of a dyad with rewards for good behavior. Punishment results from a carrot-and-a-stick or Pavlovian concepts in psychology. The belief that positive behavior must be forced, coerced, or cajoled out of inherently unruly children. Children are bribed to do good things and to make an effort, using candy and even money. Ironically punishment/bribe cycles reinforce each other. If we punish bad behavior, then we must manipulate or reward to get good behavior. They reinforce beliefs that people don't want to do work and be good.

---

71. OBSERVING
PUNISHMENT AND CONTROL

Take time to observe punishment and control around you. Notice how you feel when you are being punished. Notice what you want to do when you feel you are being punished. Notice what you actually do when you feel you are being punished. Now notice other people who appear to be punished. Notice how they respond. Notice how they react or behave. Notice the behavior of the punisher. Notice how the punisher feels.

Punishment is the fastest and easiest method. It always betrays impatience. During punishment people's feelings and their relationship to their feelings ceases to matter. This sets in motion deep patterns of automatic responses of denial, reaction, and rebellion. If the stress of the punishment is too high, the punished person may simply respond in kind. Punishment also gives attention to a child and if that is the source of much of that child's attention he will want more of it. He will do more unacceptable things just to get the attention. This may create a life-long pattern. I am amazed at how well children behave despite repeated humiliation, shame, abuse, and coercion experienced in punishment.

SIEGE MENTALITY

Many adults and institutions involved in care of children are highly addicted to punishment. A siege mentality is common in many city schools because the more that punishment and control are applied the worse the behavior crisis becomes. Many believe the problem is a result of current permissiveness. The idea of questioning the value of punishment may seem very frightening. It may be considered a new trend that will pass, and we will return to the old-fashioned maxim "spare the rod and spoil the child."

---

72. DISCUSSING PUNISHMENT AND PEACE

Have an open discussion (Insight Process) with children in your life about punishment, control, and discipline, and peace.

ASSISTING CHILDREN IN RECOGNIZING DANGER

There are obvious times in which a child's or an adult's knowledge of the world is not sufficient to protect them from a dangerous situation. A small child does not know not to go out in the middle of a busy street or not to touch a hot fire. Any observer would naturally shout "Stop!" or "Watch out!" Rather than creating lots of rules for children to anticipate disasters, we need to help children develop their perceptions so that they can make these distinctions for themselves.

I have found that, though it takes a lot of time to explain such things to children, most do want long discussions about how to be careful. In these instances I try to say something like, "I can see that you don't know that this hot fire will burn you. Feel how hot is is even when you aren't close. Imagine how hot is must be when you get close.(They may react and let you know they understand.) I know you learning quickly and next time you will will know to stay away from hot things. I care about you and want to help you to learn to take care of yourself." Even when children resist being dissuaded from harmful behavior, continue such statements, persistently, with patience. They may not seem to work, but in time the point of view will take hold. You can have these discussions with two year-olds-long before they can actually talk to you, laying the foundation for their learning about the danger. You may feel your way around. Vary your discussion: as the child becomes less responsive to one version, try another. In time the child will be willing to take responsibility for being aware of potential dangers. This awareness will grow and become more complex and subtle. Whereas, if they sense your disapproval or constant need for your protection, they will shrink and act out of fear of you as well as fear of the danger.

CONFLICTING AGENDAS

When children resist doing something that you want them to do, utilize persistent communication like: "I know you want to do this. This isn't a good time to do it but at x time you can," "I know how disappointing it is that you can't do this." Any communication that establishes a dialogue about how to have each person's needs and desires acknowledged and cared about is important. When children come to believe that their needs are not as important as those of adults, they fail to learn how to advocate for and meet their own needs, and see that these are accommodated. They also do not learn the difference between important and immediate needs. Children with repressed needs become needy adults.

When my grandson Elijah was one-and-a-half, he wanted to stay up all night. I was working at night and would bring him home late to go to sleep shortly after we arrived. Elijah would start crying. At first I thought he would cry himself to sleep. He didn't. So we talked about what we would do tomorrow and he would let go of the day and sleep knowing that tomorrow we could do things. Now he is over two, and I have found that in order to get him to fall asleep I talk to him about how much his body needs the sleep and how much fun he will have when he is rested.

Our effectiveness in working with supporting peace and dealing with conflicting wants and needs depends upon the degree with which we have dealt with our own inner neediness. Thus we can utilize this sort of interaction in dealing with others in situations in which we are asked to change plans or bend to accommodate the agenda of another. For instance: "I realize that you want me to do this right now, but this is what is going on with me."

73. PEACE CONTRACTS

Create contracts for peace between you and children. Talk about how you will each work toward achieving peace. Talk about how you will each monitor this process. You can do this with children of any age, once they start talking.

Contracts are like goals for cooperative interaction between adults or adults and children. They can be created by drawing pictures or writing down desired behavior or desired ultimate outcome. They can be part of the process of reaching a desired goal such as a toy, a college degree, a vacation, etc. They must be mutually beneficial and involve the commitment of both parties. They are not another way for parents to control children. Contracts can cover all areas of behavior. You can agree with the children you deal with on work, play, possessions, or behavior towards others. You can also contract how you will ensure that the contracts are followed and what to do when you want to change a contract.

The important ingredient in this interaction is persistence on the part of adults and willingness to work through some agreement with the child or other adult. This process may take time. Often we feel pushed to do things quickly. However, if we take the time necessary, initially, then the process becomes more habitual and agreements will be reached more quickly. Avoid using a Peace Chair or behavior contracts as a way of railroading over children's or other adult's thoughts and needs.

When we engage in making contracts with children, we are taking a step toward treating them as our equals. This may run counter to our experiences as children or the general beliefs of our society. When we learn to treat children as our equals, we start to teach them self-reliance, responsibility, and personal integrity. Within the contract relationship parents and other adults need to begin to let children experience their own desires and goals. Often when children want something and finally get it they experience disappointments, perhaps the toy breaks or the outing is not what they expected. Often we try to fix this. Because we have a hard time dealing with our own suffering, we have an even harder time dealing with the possibility of the suffering of our children. In a contract or mutually agreement, the child becomes more and more responsible for the outcome as well as the steps along the way.

CONTROL

Peace as a goal in the home or classroom is far more consistent than any goal of control. For the experience of being in control can vary from child to child, and adult to adult. Control is not a positive experience in the adult-child relationship. In this situation, the teacher or parent may be in control, but it is at the expense of the child who ultimately experiences being out-of-control. A child then attempts to reestablish a sense of control, as he often does by acting out. Acting out can be any of hundreds of strategies from temper tantrums to using various mood altering substances. But when a child tries to utilize covert or even overt means of gaining some control, the adults experience feeling out-of-control. And so a struggle for control goes on constantly. Control also facilitates miscommunication. In control oriented communicating, adults do not talk about or respond to the child's feelings.

---

74. EXPERIENCING A CONTROL DYNAMIC

Look at the world's interactions. Watch to see when people are treated or treat another, in a sense, as children. These people can be adults. They can be employer and employee, or husband and wife. Watch when one person makes a decision for another person. Notice when one person believes he has power or freedom that another doesn't. Notice how the two interact. Notice how they create a pattern of behavior toward one another. Become more and more aware when this sort of interaction occurs until you are able to see it happen in your own life. When you do, notice how you feel. Notice if you can sense how the other person may be experiencing this.

POWERLESSNESS

Once acting out begins, it seems to have a self-perpetuating dynamic. Emanating from unexpressed feelings and needs, those feelings and needs remain to further stimulate behavior. Without the capacity to express himself, one must act. A sense of powerless holds the dynamic in place, causing it to spiral onward and upward. Because an experience of being controlled and not having needs acknowledged stimulates the acting out, efforts to assert more control results in more acting out. Both the person acting out and the one controlling feel powerless as neither sees the the dynamic that is taking place.

---

75. OBSERVING POWERLESSNESS

Notice when people express powerlessness. Powerlessness means that they feel like a victim, feel life is doing things to them, feel that they have no say over their fate. Notice how they talk about themselves and the conditions of their lives. Notice how they see themselves. Notice when you communicate this way. Notice how you feel about yourself and perceive yourself.

76. FINDING PEACE IN POWER UNBALANCE

Think of a time in your life when you felt like a victim — when life was unfair or wrong and in which you were harmed. Think about experiences of being out of control, of being controlled by someone else more powerful than you, or upon whom you were dependent. Think about all details of one such event. Now relax. Ask your inner-self if it is possible to see that differently. Ask to see the lesson in that experience. Ask to see what you gained from that experience. Ask if that painful experience might also have brought you some way of changing yourself so that you could feel more powerful the next time.

A feeling of powerlessness can change so that we may gain a sense of self-understanding. Often, we feel that we have to have a better job, more status, or more physical power in order to deal with the feeling of powerlessness. When we find that we can change the feelings, we may be less driven to have to prove that we are powerful. This may alleviate school yard brawls and other confrontational relationships that arise when we feel powerless.

This is not an exercise in teaching people to accept unacceptable situations. Instead when a person is empowered in their past, they will not recreate situations in which they are the victim. By seeing the lesson or a way to forgive themselves for being so helpless, they can stop a compulsive pattern of fear of powerlessness.

---

77. OBSERVING RESPONSIBILITY

Notice when people accept responsibility and when they do not. If possible, notice how others go about doing things, how cautious, how reckless, how easy going, how natural their efforts are. Notice what happens when things go wrong. Notice what happens when things go right. Notice how people behave when painful or terrible things happen. Notice this both in your own life and throughout society.

RESPONSIBILITY

Most teachers and parents say that before you grant children freedom, they first must demonstrate responsibility. This expresses adult doubt that children are able to be responsible at all. So the moment that they act irresponsibly after we have granted them some privilege, we say, "See! I told you so."

What is responsibility anyway? And what should I be or am I responsible for? We are responsible for ourselves and our lives. Children are responsible for themselves and their lives, to the degree that they can or are allowed to care for themselves. Children may need help for a while. But all of us need help. We need to interact with each other in jobs and in the thousands of events that take place in our lives. Children are given shelter and nurturing until they can start the process of sheltering themselves. Nurturing will always be a human need, regardless of the chronological age.

To what degree am I responsible for my life? You are absolutely responsible. The understanding of our ultimate responsibility for our lives comes slowly to us as our awareness grows.

Until we accept responsibility for both our failures and triumphs, we live as victims of life. When we can see that our lives are unfolding a pattern of wisdom and personal mastery, then we have achieved the ultimate responsibility.

It is in the grey area between absolute responsibility and partial responsibility that we do not wish to be responsible for our lives. It is in this grey area that we see ourselves as powerless, victims, as smaller than the vast the universe. We appear powerless in the face of the myriad of things that happen on planet Earth. Yet if we are willing to seize hold of all of our lives, we can slowly narrow or eliminate this grey area in which we do not believe we control our lives. If I believe I am responsible for everything in my life, then I must be capable of truly great things. This is because I have much to do with the world and my interactions with it.

WE ARE RESPONSIBLE
FOR SEEING OTHERS AS RESPONSIBLE

How can we punish others for not being responsible when we have not taken responsibility for everything that takes place in our own lives? When we interact with children or other adults, we can choose to see them as capable or incapable. If we see people as failures at living some "normal" or "ideal" life, we disempower them. If we see people as capable of taking care of their own problems, we are furthering the process of their doing so. All people have the capacity to find solutions through which they can grow as humans toward greater love and understanding of themselves and others. And when we see this, we will also see it in ourselves.

If we have a clear sense of where we stop and others start, then it becomes easier for us to be responsible for our lives. Talking about our boundaries and how it feels when others invade our sense of our own space is a good Insight Process exercise — particularly when dealing with responsibility.

78. BOUNDARY GAME

This can be a game for children, a practice in forming and experiencing boundaries. Have them pretend that they have a force field (like in science fiction movies) around their bodies that protects them. Let them practice how close they will allow others to come to their force fields. Tell them to warn other children when they get too close to the force field.

RESPONSIBILITY, CHOICE, AND BOUNDARIES

Asking children to consider themselves responsible for their own lives works when we acknowledge that they are totally in charge of everything about themselves. This may seem heretical because they can't support themselves: at least few do in our culture. Though in tribal cultures children are often self-sufficient as early as 10 years of age. These kids make choices in every area of their lives. For our children these choices need to be the ones that they can make at that point or age in their participation in family, school and society. Thus a very small child can help decide what to have for dinner, what to have in his or her bedroom, and perhaps even where to go to nursery school or child care. (Please note that these are also boundary issues. His responsibilities have to do with his life.) An older child can be allowed to decide on school and classroom whenever possible, as well as how and when he or she makes a contribution (work) to the family, community, and school (ie homework). Much discussion needs to evolve in these work decisions, so that the older child can see that choice is not whether or not to work. The main ingredient is patient and ongoing conversations from toddlers onward. Having been reared in unilateral ways, I realize how difficult it is to change old patterns of deciding everything for children.

For adults involved with children this may amount to a slow process of letting go of conducting children's lives for them. But we can see how this attitude has already pervaded thinking about infants. In early editions of Dr. Spock's guides to child-rearing, parents were to insure that infants we getting a balance of baby food. In recent editions the approach is to allow infants to choose the food that they want to eat and that the balance will come about naturally. This comes from the assumption that infants know what is good for them and what they need to ensure their physical health. They have an internal awareness that is the basis for their communications about eating. This can also be seen in the practice of feeding them on demand, rather than on a rigid schedule as was the case 40 years ago. Parents may have problems relating to the idea that children may in fact have an awareness of needs. Parents may fear an endlessly demanding infant. Yet when allowed to choose and indicate their preferences, infants are much more content and learn and develop in ways which are natural for them.

CHILDREN AS EXPERTS ON THEMSELVES

Children at a very early age need to learn that they are the sole authority on what they choose to feel and experience. This is their own domain. Their self-image and choices are their own province. This is the most powerful realization that anyone can help a child grasp. Once a child sees how much control he has over his thinking, he can begin to notice how the thinking is the basis for his acts upon the world, and finally upon how the world acts upon him.

Understanding that children are the sole authority over themselves can be emphasized with regard to their bodies. A child who believes he is in charge of his body can tell others not to treat this body in uncomfortable ways. A parent or teacher who believes this and allows children to develop and learn this point will find that these children will be far less likely to have problems with physical and sexual abuse, acting out through taking drugs or other substances, and acting out through sexual promiscuity or early pregnancies. If adults do not believe deeply in their own responsibility for their bodies, it is difficult for them to teach it with conviction.

PEACE AND RESPONSIBILITY

Peace is a choice. It is a choice we can make with regard to the goals of our families, social groups, and our schools. When we don't choose peace, we often choose to control others in order to have things go smoothly. When we choose to control others, we lose track of boundaries — ours and theirs. We get into conflict and carrot-and-stick approaches to group, family, and school goals. Pursuing peace often means pursuing responsibility and honoring who we are. If we can agree to a peaceful classroom, school, and family, we can talk about attaining that goal. It is one that we can continue to work toward day in and day out. From my own experience when we work with peace as a goal, we add fulfillment, cooperation, and success to our lives.

8. COOPERATION

Public schools have recently been trying to introduce the idea
of cooperation — possibly fueled by the realization that Japanese
work "teams" have given Japan a competitive economic edge. It
is also, of course, part of a changing understanding of society, in
which cooperation in businesses is seen as part of competition.
We find it in sports teams and in the so-called "team spirit" in businesses. In today's jargon the use of cooperation is called a "win-
win" situation which still is the language of competition. This
muddies the waters around the idea of cooperation, somehow
convincing us that we can strive for both competition and cooperation at the same time. Yet our ability to compete is damaged
when we look to the success of everyone. Cooperation and competition are based in very different attitudes toward human behavior. Competition focuses upon the individual accomplishment. I take care of my own needs, and you take care of yours.
If I excel in competition, my accomplishments will be more fully
acknowledged than someone else's. While cooperation involves
interactive behavior in which the goals, wants, and needs of individuals are understood to be similar to those of others within the
group. When we cooperate, we find ways of taking care of our
personal needs within the context of supporting and working
with others.

In this century, many social scientists have based their model
for human behavior in the concept of "the survival of the fittest."
According to that model, competition was the reason for human
advances and for the success of our species. The most successful competitors went on to have their genes and points of view
replicated. Today the survivalist model is being replaced by a realization that humans are social and depend upon interaction
with others for their very existence. The cooperative model of
human evolution suggests that we have survived because we
have cooperated. In this model, a little bit of competition may not
be destructive to a person's self-image, but a society of relentless
competition produces a few "winners" and a large disaffected
population. Being an "also ran" does not necessarily lead to
high estimates of self-worth. Ironically, winning does not necessarily lead to high self-esteem, either. Heavily competitive human

interaction can lead to a climate of conflict, low moral, and disaffection or alienation.

Competition seems so much a part of our society, "the American way," that it is hard to imagine social forms that do not include competition as the central human behavior. Competition is so prevalent in every aspect of public life that even if we concentrate upon developing cooperative groups and approaches, these will be cast in the light of our traditional love affair with competition. And frequently we run up against the following dilemma: "'How can I go for this promotion when I know that "team mate," who has also applied for the promotion, will not get it if I do? Maybe I have to design work situations in which we all get to advance, together."

79. OBSERVING COMPETITION AND COOPERATION

Observe competition and cooperation in groups, individuals, etc. Notice how you define and think about competition and cooperation. Watch groups interacting. Watch sports teams. Watch work groups. Watch social groups. Watch all instances of group interactions. Observe both the benefits people seem to be deriving and the anxiety and conflict that they are experiencing from either cooperation or competition. Notice when group interaction is working and when it seems not to be working well. Notice when people are interacting cooperatively and competitively. See if you can tell the difference between the two. Notice the kinds of behavior involved. Notice the kinds of communication involved in cooperation and competition. Do this exercise frequently, each time you will learn something new.

FAMILIES AND COOPERATION

Our family is the primary source for ideas about about group interaction, sex roles and behavior. Our families are the templates from which we evolve as social beings. Without the family's powerful efforts to be cooperative, this society would degenerate into alienated individuals scraping for pieces of the economic and social pie, with each person fending for himself. Because much of our economic interaction is highly competitive, when politicians call for a return to family values they are unconsciously responding to the cooperative function of families. Families offer a refuge from highly competitive public forms of interaction.

Remember your experience of group interaction and cooperation in your own family.

80. OBSERVING COOPERATION IN FAMILY LIFE

Notice cooperative patterns in your family and other families with whom you interact. What qualities does this cooperation depend upon? What sort of beliefs sustain cooperation? Which beliefs do not support cooperative interaction? Notice your own beliefs? How important is cooperation between family members to you? What sort of behaviors are good for cooperation? Which behaviors undermine cooperation? How do you feel when your family is cooperative? How do you feel when it is not being cooperative? How would you define "cooperation" in terms of what you see in families? Try to make a new definition of "cooperation" based in your ongoing observations.

81. FAMILY COOPERATION II

Answer the following. What did cooperation in your family feel like? Who got to make the rules? Who seemed to have the most power and or control? Who took care of people? Who paid attention to feelings? How were your needs met? How did you meet other family members' needs? How did you get a sense of togetherness and unity? How did you get a sense of closeness and love? If you were to make changes in your family, what would they be?

Careful use of these two exercises over a period of time should help to focus upon our needs within groups and expectations of groups. Insight gained will help in working toward strengthening and supporting cooperative interactions in our lives. We can see what we learned from our family to sustain our relationships with others, particularly our important intimate relationships.

82. CREATING YOUR VISION
OF A COOPERATIVE GROUP

(Guided process.) See yourself in a small valley beside a beautiful lake. The valley is filled with beautiful flowers. You can hear a cool breeze as it moves through the trees. You are here with a group of people. This is your life empowerment group. Watch how you work with one another -to eat and care for your bodies, to care for your home, to care for your children and parents your sisters, your brothers, your friends, those who you admire, and your teachers. See in your mind's eye how each person treats one another. See how they treat you and your needs for nurturing and for satisfying life work and life relationships. Experience how it feels to work, play, and live with such a group. How free do you feel? Do you feel that what you do matters to the other members of the group? Does what they do matter to you? Out of the heart of this group comes a wise older brother or sister. He or she comes up to you and whispers into your ear a goal: that you can keep in your heart that will help you to create such a group in your life. You come out of the beautiful valley and back to where you are. You write down your goal and read it every day.

PROBLEMS IN COOPERATIVE INTERACTION

Cooperative interaction runs up against each person's fear of being out-of-control, fear of having someone else try to take control over his or her life. When we were infants, we had to depend upon someone for our survival. We survived. Many of us have issues with how we were treated as we survived. Yet that parent was, by and large, doing his or her best out of his or her capacity to be nurturing and support our survival. Because we have not forgotten the feeling of being overwhelmed by another's control over our lives, we often live in a state of constant anxiety and fear over both our survival and our integrity. We have complex memories of how dependent we were. These memories interact with unconscious patterns. Thus as we get close a bell goes off in our mind and our fear of dependency is triggered. When we get too distant from others another bell goes off and we recall all of the feelings that came up when we wandered too far from mother or father's protection. We often are thrown between two unacceptable poles being smothered or being alienated.

Our fear of being absorbed by another's identity is why individualism and competition have such appeal. Yet we know on some deeper level that we need each other. (By "deeper level" I mean that it is not necessarily a part of our conscious day by day thoughts. It's just a feeling deep within, an intuition or, perhaps, a longing for closeness.) It is as frightening for us to feel ourselves to be this separate from everyone as it is to feel that they might take control over our lives. In developing self-esteem we learn to understand these two forces within, the push and the pull. We learn to be in harmony with our uniqueness and our need for closeness.

SELF-ESTEEM AND COOPERATION

Developing cooperative behavior depends upon developing a strong sense of self-love. If we love and trust ourselves, then we do not feel so threatened by the attempts of others to control us. We can say "no" or "yes" to demands and pressures that group interaction brings according to our compassion toward ourselves. If we can see that another person's needs and survival are not all that different from ours, the two of us can work together on our mutual needs and survival. People do this when they marry. Yet we need more than just a husband and wife relationship in a world as vast, complex, and populous as this.

At one time people were aligned in clans, consisting of intricate and extensive family connections. They were animated by the push and pull of intimacy and integrity just as marriages are. To the degree that the members of the clans took care of each other's needs and survival, they were helpful. To the degree that clans struggled and competed against the needs and survival of other clans, they strengthened distrust of others. Clans or tribes often saw other clans as aliens or different and projected the problems and suffering that they experienced on the other clans. Through creating scapegoats outside of the clan, they held the group together. But this also weakened self-love and created greater distrust amongst those who clung together against this outside threat.

Today we can develop interactive groups, beyond the marriage partner, clan, or family, in which we strengthen self-love along with trust of one another. We live on a shrinking planet, and whether we wish to or not we will interact with people very different from those who lived in our family group. Modern communication technology shows the effect each one of us has upon other people living on this planet, whether it has to do with polluting the planet or with the economic flow back and forth. We can see how a decision to buy a certain fast food leads to the destruction of a rainforest. In newspaper article, or television image, we see further how the loss of a rainforest affects the climate and atmosphere. Thus my cooperative interaction with another person in a group is a template, just as my experience of my family was a template, for the cooperative interaction of all others on the planet. If I learn to care about the members of my group, in time I can learn to care about those who live at great distance from me in the rainforest. My capacity to empathize expands past differences within my group to include people who don't speak the same language or live in the same manner. What I learn about nurturing and supporting other people I will pass on to others by my example. What I learn about alienating and hostile behavior I pass along as well.

GOAL STATEMENTS FOR COOPERATION

Most of us have cooperative experiences in friendship groups and in the family. We need now to build these experiences into models of ever more empowering and supportive group structures. A cooperative group may grant the following qualities to its members:

1. High self-worth (self-esteem)

2. A sense of personal integrity that works with membership. I belong to myself. I have chosen to be part of this group, and in being part I am part of your life and you are part of mine.

3. A feeling of caring about one another beyond the need to use one another's skills and abilities and characteristics. I am willing to be aware of your feelings, your pain, and your joy. I appreciate your abilities but do not feel that I have the right to own them, buy them, or sell them.

4. The freedom to express one's feelings and needs.

5. A sense of being able to be responsible for oneself and for one's experience of the group. That is, knowing that my feelings are mine and that your feelings are yours. I will do the part that I have accepted as mine in our mutual agreements. I will trust that you will do your part.

6. The understanding that in supporting and nurturing you and caring about your well-being I am not abandoning my well-being or substituting yours for mine or making a trade off. I care about your well-being because I care about mine. I am not sacrificing myself and my well-being for you and yours.

You may think of additional qualities that you would want your cooperative group to have. When working with your cooperative group, it is very helpful to keep in mind the goals for the quality of interaction that you would like to achieve. Read these six descriptions or any additions to your group each time you meet. In time the belief that you can achieve this level of cooperation will become common in the group, and the group will act accordingly. Empowerment and full participation are basic goals, but each of us has barriers and personal issues that we must confront in order to realize our full potential for cooperation.

BARRIERS TO COOPERATIVE GROUP WORK

1. DIFFERENCES
We are different from nearly everybody. We feel particularly different from people of other races, nationalities, or gender. While these differences make us unique, our similarities to other people are the basis for our successful interaction with them. The basic principle for any successful cooperative interaction is our realization that, despite differences, we can care about others and can work with them.

2. RIVALRIES
When we work with children or even other adults, one of the primary areas of conflict comes out of experiences of sibling rivalry. For a variety of reasons, children often feel that they must compete with brothers and sisters for adult (e.g., parental) love

and attention. Sibling rivalry can happen even when an unrelated child threatens that child's primacy in adult eyes. When we start developing cooperative situations with children or adults we need to acknowledge this dynamic. To help children deal with competition for attention, keep these group goals: 1. Each participant's contribution is valued. 2. We all have abilities and contributions that are central to the completion of the group work. 3. Without each member, the group is incomplete. 4. Just because we let someone else be the center of attention, our needs and contributions will not be ignored or lost. A cooperative effort grows in power as we come to understand that each participant's involvement is irreplaceable.

3. CONTROL

Control strategies are diverse, arising from our fear of being controlled. We attempt to control in order to defend ourselves from being controlled. Many traditional strategies can be used by one or several members of any group to co-opt the total group effort in order to feel more in control:

MODELS OF CONTROL

A. THE AUTHORITARIAN MODEL:

Each of our lives have been deeply touched by the authoritarian model pervasive in our society. It runs counter to our efforts toward democracy. For the most part education, and traditional family forms maintain some aspects of authoritarian structure. For instance the father as head of the family who makes all of the decisions, and the teacher in charge of the classroom makes all decisions for the class. Thus trying to create a cooperative group in a school or family may run up against the habit of having one person make the majority of decisions. Sometimes authority is based in specialized knowledge or membership in a powerful group. For instance, doctors have been granted much authority over the processes of healing via the American Medical Association, insurance companies, and various laws.

Often authoritarian leaders issue orders through a chain of command to people at the bottom. The lack of feedback in the chain of command insulates the authoritarian leader from people beneath him. This is called one-way communication; feedback in highly authoritarian groups occurs as rebellion, sabotage, passive-aggressive behavior, and acting out. Group efforts are sabotaged and pro-ductivity is severely affected by lack of true inner motivation. In au-thoritarian groups, we do things because we are coerced. Author-itarian groups must have very large carrots and very large sticks. While people may continue to do their best without huge rewards, many drop out or only do as much as they are rewarded for. Scape-goats are also used, so that individuals can project responsibility for problems by focusing the dissatisfaction and low group commitment upon an outsider or enemy (for business it could be a contractor, supplier, client, etc.) of the group rather than confronting the au-thoritarian leader. I have been in several classrooms where a child becomes the scapegoat and the focus for much of the hostility and frustration of the other students.

B. CLIQUES.

The clique is an alternative to the authoritarian model. Close friends or associates may tend to take control of group interactions and become leaders as a team in self appointed-ways. Certain children may already, by virtue of their desire to please adults or to excel, have a tendency to take over for the adult authority structure, replacing it with their peer clique. Children learn to form control-oriented cliques quite early, even by kindergarten. Often, children make up rules for membership in cliques (e.g. gangs). The rules reflect their desire to be included in a group that makes their individual presence more powerful and protects them from attack or the disempowering behavior of others. These may be seen as the modern equivalent to clan group membership.

C. DROPPING OUT, WITHDRAWAL

These are also control strategies. "If I can't be in control, I will be uncontrollable," is the point of view that a drop-out takes. This gives him/her the feeling of power in a situation reminiscent of his lack of power in other group interactions. This is also called "passive-aggressive" behavior, that is, the person tries to control by resisting. Saying "no" often seems the only power one has, particularly when he or she is being coerced.

The above are a few of the control forms you will find in group formation. Now check out the sort of groups with which you in-teract and how you feel when you do.

83. OBSERVING
GROUP CONTROL STRATEGIES

Observe group interactions. Notice the control issues. Who wants to take over control of the group? How are they successful? How are they unsuccessful? Why? Who gives up, opts out? What happens when people push or pull out of a group? What happens when several people want to control? Notice how you feel toward each strategy you observe. Notice if you feel anger, rebellious, upset, hurt, sad, like giving up, like saying "no!," etc.

84. CONTROL CHECK

Watch yourself when you are working in a group. See if and how you want to take control. See how much control you ultimately want to exercise. Ask yourself why you want this control? Utilize your ongoing answers to understand your work with groups.

CONTROL VERSUS DEMOCRACY

The dynamic between wanting control and feeling out-of-control needs to be continuously recognized and discussed in any cooperative group interaction, even with very young children. The ideal of a cooperative group is democratic. As a society, we have the ideal of democracy: as individuals we often have few interactions in which each person's contribution (vote) is as important as another person's. Thus in developing cooperative groups, we place the goal of democracy as primary. We discuss how effective we are at achieving it, what our problems in interacting with each other democratically have been, and how we can solve these problems. Communication exercises such as the Insight Process are helpful in keeping open communication against the group tendency to exert pressure toward conformity (another control strategy), toward having a leader who can outvote others, or toward maintaining the status quo.

Many of us come from communication structures in which stasis or stability (control) is bought at very high cost in terms of emotional openness. That is, we are often asked to abandon our our own feelings and integrity for the sake of the group. Thus cooperative endeavors need to have open communication forms so that individual members can have the freedom necessary to express concerns and ensure that their needs and feelings are considered.

BARRIERS TO DEMOCRACY

Ideally democracies empower each member — one person, one vote. Co-opting or disempowering are strategies that counteract democracy.

CO-OPTING POWER AND DISEMPOWERING

These are forms of group interaction strategies commonly experienced by those who belong to less powerful groups such as children, women, minorities, and lower economic groups. An individual's power is co-opted by an assumed characteristic, cliche', or authority strategy, such as, "All women/blacks/children/ seniors /poor people do such and such." Thus an individual is not allowed to express a feeling or opinion, or take an action because the group or authority has decided that they know in advance what that will be. The person is seen to be part of the group by virtue of a proxy, such as a parent, spouse, friend, or someone who is a member of a more acceptable group. The individual's vote is not seen as a full vote, equal to that of others. We have moved a long way toward becoming aware of ageism, sexism, and racism. But it will be a long time before they are completely eradicated.

In schools, I have found stereotypes and bigotry expressed by children with regard to the opposite sex as well as minority groups. Boys are separated from their feelings with remarks like "Boys don't have feelings;" and girls from the contribution that they make to adults with "Girls are always teacher's pets." The power of their being, is taken from them, and they are left as partial beings —boys without an emotional life and girls without legitimate interaction with more powerful adults.

When power is contested, the tendency to disempower increases as a way of diverting energy and attention, and of gaining control over a group or social interaction. If we are arguing over who gets to leave the classroom first and the issue of girls as pets is brought up, this may change the outcome.

Adults disempower children by assuming that they cannot deal with various problems. Once children can express themselves they need to be given the opportunity to decide whether they are able to do various things and make a variety of decisions affecting their lives.

All forms of negativity are disempowering, whether it is criticism, denial, lack of support, belittling, impatience, playing mental games, or any of dozens of irresponsible interaction tactics. This behavior is the result of the poor self-esteem of the self-appointed critic who believes it makes her/him seem more important or powerful than the other person. It is also a defensive maneuver. A person decides to take control over the interaction and protect him/herself from potential criticism by criticizing first. We tend to disempower others when we fear loosing control of our lives, or fear being exposed or being seen as less important and less powerful than someone else.

85. OBSERVING DISEMPOWERING STRATEGIES

Notice when you or others use disempowering strategies to influence control and power. See how people talk to one another in ways so that one person gets a bigger vote. Notice how people position themselves with regard to groups or authority figures in order to gain a bigger vote. Notice how they manage to ensure that others do not get to vote or have a smaller vote under these circumstances. By "vote," I mean the opportunity to decide, to make the choices that will be made or need to be made. Notice ways in which participant's views and efforts are made to seem less important and less valid. Notice how individuals attempt to get others to participate in the process of invalidating certain individuals. Notice how individuals use negativity to attempt to get a majority or a core group or consensus for their way of doing things, or believing, or viewing situations.

Complaining and projecting guilt or blame onto others is also a way to disempower one another and any process. Telling people not to complain does not settle this. They need a safe space in which to express apprehension and fears that lie behind the complaints and projections. If we assume responsibility for another person's complaints or fears we continue the disempowerment. We all have the answers to all of our own problems. Others can support us while we find the answers and deal with the problems. But our problems are our own.

CONTROL AND GROUP SIZE

Virginia Satir has pointed out that an interaction that is larger than two people no longer permits the same quality of participation that one with two people creates. With the addition of more people the interaction becomes more complex, and there is more possibility that the contributions of some participants will be excluded. Even in dealing with our own children, when there is more than one, the children become anxious about being neglected and included. This concern amplifies for children in classrooms of 20 to 30 children. It is not possible for teachers to have the quality interaction with students that parents in small families can have. It is necessary for teachers to turn this function over to the children themselves. However, as so much in the classroom has to do with control, it may often seem impossible for the teacher to relinquish that much control.

Here's an exercise that will graphically demonstrates control issues in any group including a family.(1.) Children like this physical type of exercise.

---

86. SATIR'S CONTROL DYNAMIC EXERCISE

Tie a rope to all members of a group so that they are linked together. Now have one member pull on the rope. Now another member pulls on the rope and so forth. After you have done this, talk about how it feels to be pulled on and to pull. How does it feel to be caught up in the rope and what can you do to change this? Translate this to how people respond to rules, instructions, and other methods for exerting control in groups and in society. Talk about alternatives to this.

87. HOW DO I DO IN A GROUP ?

Use this as a guided process with eyes closed. Imagine yourself in a group that you normally deal with. See how you feel. How do you interact with the members of that group? What are your feelings about yourself when you deal with each member of that group? Now see yourself interacting with these people individually. How do you feel now? What is this relationship like? Slowly go through each interaction. Now see your ideal group relationship. What does it feel like? How are the members of this group relating to you?

ABC'S OF GROUP FORMATION

1. GROUP SUCCESS:

To be successful, a group in the home, business, or at school must have as its primary goal the success of everyone in the group. Equality of success can mean that each member may define what success looks like to him or her. If the goal of the group is not everybody's success, then the group will start out of the gate with inherent conflict. One conflict might be that the group success is important but an individual's is not. Another conflict might be that one's success is a goal but another's is not. Most groups are formed to do a specific task. Without the unifying goal of success for each, there will be dozens of conflicting subgoals. Reaching the goal will become more and more difficult as each person works toward his or her subgoal. Some participants may not care whether the goal is reached; others will want to prevent their enemies from participating. Each participant in the project needs to believe that he is as central as anyone else to the success of the project before he will focus his energy on it.

2. VISION

Creating a deep understanding that individuals are working within the group toward a common group end will give any activity the necessary vision to power it forward. We all want to make a positive contribution to life. For instance, a political party calls upon its vision of democracy for all to unite members of the party. Attention to the needs and dreams of individuals can unite a group. The goal of group activity must be an umbrella under which everyone can stand with integrity and honesty. Thus short term individual goals such as getting a good grade or an allowance do not serve to create an umbrella for a group effort.

The reward and punishment dynamic fragments group efforts. Group punishment is extremely difficult to assess or apply. Who is responsible? Members begin to focus upon blaming one another and the group falls apart. Punishment rarely creates more than coerced group activity.

Group work goes forward more effectively when tasks are collected under a common understanding. For instance, a child would be more willing to participate in household tasks if he saw that this allowed all members of the home more time to contribute to life — if he knew of or understood the vision that animates his parent's lives and how important the parents contribution was to this vision. Often, we do not take the time to talk to children about the deep and meaningful purposes in our lives. When we do so it helps us to again anchor our lives in our personal vision.

3. PERSONAL VISION
Find a way to have the group vision work with individual personal visions. The desire to contribute is very deep within each of us. As we reach to those depths, we will find commonality that unites our individual visions into the group goal.

4. PERSONAL GROWTH AND UNDERSTANDING
The ideal group form is one in which participants gain intrinsic benefits from the group itself, benefits that go beyond the project or goal. Again, we need to develop ongoing group interaction processes so that problems can be successfully understood and solved. Problems that come up in group work are no different from problems we each have as individuals. For even with a positive umbrella, goal problems will come up and conflicts will occur. However, with a goal of success for all, the format for approaching the conflicts is set. As we deal with problems and conflicts, we realize that solving them will lead to each person gaining skills at working with their own problems and with future group problems.

5. DEMOCRACY AND GROUP STRUCTURE

Because our current efforts toward democracy are recent (200 years in human history is a short time), we are still attempting to find forms that work.

A. CONSENSUS

Consensus is an agreement achieved by discussions or work that minimizes the number and/or degree of dissension. That is, consensus has been achieved when there is minimal disagreement with this way of doing things. When placed under a vision umbrella, there may be a temptation to overrun disagreement with expediency. However, vision also helps to place disagreement in perspective. Very small picky changes in ways of doing things may not look appropriate in comparison to the vision.

B. VOTING

A common way to move things forward in a democracy is by voting. There are parliamentary rules that help to organize voting, but these depend upon having officers and leaders. We vote on how things are being done constantly through our criticism and support. Voting sometimes brings people's positions out into the open. Voting also assumes that all are equal as each has the same vote. Voting has less value in a group where one person is given a veto (Cf disempowerment and authoritarian groups).

C. LEADERS

Any time a group designates a leader, who has more power than other members, it is moving away from learning to become truly cooperative. Yet at the beginning of forming cooperative groups, it may be nearly impossible to function without a leader. If it is possible, pass leadership from one member to another equally. Participants can talk about leadership versus membership and come to have a sense of how to have leaders without losing the cooperative interaction of members.

D. COORDINATOR

Often it is difficult to ensure that people remain responsible for tasks throughout the overall work of a group. Delegating responsibility and keeping track of who is suppose to do what is the job of a coordinator. At times the coordinator becomes the surrogate leader of the group. In cooperative groups, traditional leadership roles such as coordinator may be constantly rotated so that the accrued power and experience are shared.

E. FACILITATOR

The optimal leadership approach is a facilitation, which literally means someone who makes things easy. A facilitator, whose goal is the success of each participant of the group, makes all work or participation happen naturally and with ease. In this regard, it is the ultimate support function and not really a leadership position in that it follows, and encourages the flow of interaction, energy, work, and achievement.

The best work of teachers and parents when developing cooperative learning and group work is as a facilitator. Many parents and teachers do this naturally. By facilitating the development of integrity, responsibility, trust, and various other qualities valuable in interpersonal relationships, they can let children function autonomously in complete confidence. Adults are thereby released from stress and worry and a need to control. When children see that they can create functioning groups which serve them well, they gain confidence in themselves so that their relationship with adults becomes more cooperative as well.

6. RESPONSIBILITY

Taking responsibility for one's own life is the centerpiece of self-knowledge. We often want to take responsibility for our successes but not our failures. This leads to a split in our self-understanding, for in the so-called failures are lessons which are the seeds for future growth and successes. Because we tend to label failure "bad" and success "good," we polarize the learning process. Cooperative work can move toward less rigid value systems so that participants can learn from the group process. Often in working with children, self-appointed monitors will spring up to tell us who is doing things "wrong." Dealing with the value systems that these monitors guard can be part of group learning, and can be worked with in Insight Process discussions. It is optimal not to grade children in cooperative groups, either as a group or as individuals, for this denies the value of learning and growth in and of themselves. It also pits children or adults against each other and breaks down the cooperative quality. Poor group grades can lead to blame and attempts at internal reprisals as happens with group punishment. If the task is accomplished, the reward is there. The project itself can be graded.

When we each can know that we are the source for all that is in our lives, particularly the way we view our lives, then we have achieved a level of responsibility that is totally liberating. We have set ourselves free, mentally, to do anything, to achieve any goal that is ours to pursue. In our inner world, when we cease to blame everyone else for our sorrows and suffering and choose to live joyously, we will know for certain that the end to all pain is possible. Until then, we can learn to view our acts as responsibly as possible — learning to correct ourselves when we have consciously violated the integrity of others and noticing it when we have unconsciously abandoned our self-love.

7. FREEDOM

Groups can nurture the freedom to be oneself. The task of a group often may seem to demand specific ways of doing the work. Yet, if the group can recognize that each of us is by his or her very nature unique and irreplaceable, then the energy of individuals will more easily be focused upon the task, perhaps even creating work forms that are more effective. Not every member will be functioning at the same level nor have the same technical or intellectual skills. Self-esteem demands that we acknowledge that we are valid regardless of work, status, appearance, or possessions. We all are legitimate beings on this earth, every last one of us. When we do what our deepest feelings tell us to do, we experience the power and freedom inherent in being ourselves, fully and completely. Often in perfectionist compulsions, teachers, parents, and adult groups feel that each task should be done perfectly. This inhibits experimentation and often demands that things continue to be done in out-of-date ways. Play is much freer than any education work. Use the role of play to guide the formation of cooperative group work. Let us play at it and learn as we go.

8. TRUST

To function democratically and utilize the skills and abilities of all participants, group members will learn that they must cultivate trust. Trust is part of responsibility — trusting each other's opinions and contributions and deepest motivations, trusting that members will do what they say they will. So often we want responsibility from others, but we don't want to trust them. And so we are always second guessing and checking on them from a nontrusting belief system. This undermines the total effort. It often seems to place members of a group at odds with one another, trying to prove their worthiness, trying to show each other that they are OK. A lot of energy is expended in checking on other people's contribution and on proving that the untrustworthy beliefs are well or poorly founded. We can demonstrate our trust to be justified as easily as we can show that our distrust has a basis in fact. The climate around the two approaches is radically different. Trust is supportive and nurturing. Distrust is hostile and disempowering.

9. INTEGRITY:

Integrity matters. Integrity seems to be a word that combines trust and responsibility. As we each polish our individual integrity, our ability to be truthful about where we are, what we are doing, and how we feel at any given moment, we will find that cooperative efforts become smoother and more straightforward. Nothing slows processes or work down like efforts to hide the truth about ourselves. We then put an enormous amount of effort into disguising and denying. Children, especially when very young, have not yet learned as much guile and self-deception as most adults practice. Thus their attempts toward integrity need to be honored. When they talk about problems of lack of fairness or lack of honesty, we need to learn to acknowledge that they do see where problems lie. Adults working with children tend to be directive and projective rather than talking truthfully about themselves. Adults are patronizing in believing that they do not need to have integrity and be honest about fears and feelings, when dealing with children.

10. COMMITMENT

Like all of the characteristics of cooperative groups such as democracy or integrity, commitment grows as the cooperative nature of the group develops. It is difficult to commit to a group in which one's integrity and individuality are ignored, in which one's well-being and contribution are neglected. We all make various levels of commitment to life and to our groups depending upon what we think of as "trade offs." That is, "If I do this, then they must do that." This is often the case in employment. Yet employees often have so little commitment that they care little about whether the enterprise for which they work survives. As members of a cooperative group find the freedom and openness to express themselves and to insure that their abilities and needs are respected, commitment will grow. A group with a high degree of commitment of all its members can powerfully change the world. Near total commitment can only be brought from positive goals and vision. Negative goals such as the desire to control people or control business enterprises cannot elicit more than the "trade off" variety of commitment.

Children have the same capacity to commit that adults have. Often children do not withhold their enthusiasm and efforts, but play or work for all they are worth. Nurturing their intense involvement in a cooperative group work will give them experiences and skills to take forward into the many groups with which they will be involved throughout their lives.

11. EXPERIMENTATION

In learning to create cooperative groups experimentation is necessary. Children can learn to make up rules for group activity based in their personal sense of what would be cooperative. Part of the growth process for adults will be to learn to trust that children can create appropriate structures for cooperation.

12. SELF-MONITORING

Learning cooperation is a process that compliments the initial purpose of the group. The process will push to the surface the dynamics of multiple relationships. Within a goal of success many issues and problems will arise. A self-monitoring cooperative group will allow time for different points of view in the group work, for feedback, and for dealing with issues. Part of the vision and growth aspects of a cooperative group is to learn from the interactions and functioning of its members. As we learn from this process, we learn to create groups that better serve and achieve success.

88. SELF-MONITORING

At intervals during your cooperative group efforts, stop and self-monitor. Take the following inventory. Write down your thoughts about each point and then disscuss the points as a group. 1. What expectations do you have for this project? 2. What fears and apprehensions do you have for working as a group on the project and for the project itself? 3. How do you feel about how you are doing in the project and group? 4. How do you feel about how the rest of the group is doing on the project and as a group? 5. What do you feel is not working and you would change? How would you change it? How do you think others would want to change it? How do you know what others might want to change? 6. What do you like about what you and the group are doing? How would you want to support continuing the parts that are good?

89. BASIC VALUES IN INTERACTIONS

Do this exercise separately for the various concepts: Democracy, Integrity, Commitment, Freedom, Trust, Responsibility, Success. Write the word at the top of two pieces of paper.(For very young children, an adult or older child can write or draw pictures on a board or paper for them.) On one paper write (discuss) what is good about this concept when people use it. On the other write what problems happen when people are involved with this concept, what apprehensions and what fears you have about it. Now list ways that you and the group might ensure that you support the positive values of these concepts. List ways of achieving greater integrity, commitment, responsibility, etc., and ways of dealing with the fears and apprehensions that you have noticed when you are asked to be more trusting. In the group, try to come up with a group definition for the concepts. Try again in a few months or so.

WHY COOPERATIVE GROUPS?

If a cooperative group does not have the ingredients for satisfying relationships with people and the potential working in productive and fulfilling ways, then you may still need the security of a known authoritarian structure. If you feel that you must defend authoritarian forms, then don't embark upon trying to create cooperative relationships until you can see their value.

The advantage of cooperative learning situations for children is actually what we each expect for children. We expect that all of our children will be loved and respected in a fairly equal manner. We would each bristle if we took our children to some group or some sport and the leader said; "We are going to love slender red-heads (straight black hair) with 120 (140) plus I.Q. better than the other children. We are going to give them all the fun jobs and the positive feedback. Your child must make do with second, third or fourth best." We expect our children to be treated equally in school and to be assisted in every possible way to learn and to grow into happy, healthy people who like themselves. We believe that all children have the potential to be successful and fulfilled in life.

FORMING A COOPERATIVE GROUP
FOR FUN AND WORK AT HOME OR SCHOOL:

Nearly every task can be done by more than one person, even if it is customarily done by only one. We can even brush each other's teeth if we wish to. When we start using cooperative groups, it may take a while to learn to share the tasks. Tasks are often considered good and bad. Children may be concerned about fairness, who does what, how they will be rewarded and ac-knowledged for their contributions, how they will decide how to do the job, and about some people getting things their way. It may seem initially that much talk and time is consumed debating these issues. I would suggest that you use the Insight Process. Adults may feel that they don't have time or patience for this de-bate. This may particularly seem to be the case in classrooms where a certain curriculum must be covered. Adults might see the process of teaching and learning cooperative group work an-other task, like doing the dishes every night or a math lesson. In time children will be able to form and execute cooperative group structures. If other groups of children are doing this, they can take time to compare notes and try new things.

When starting to work with cooperative groups you may want to start with tasks or projects that already have a group context. Social studies is a good subject from the fourth grade on. Take part of a subject or an enjoyable task and have the group work around it. Small groups are best initially, groups of three to five. As the children's' skills grow, increase the group size, and continue to experiment with the dynamic. In time children and adults can learn to function in cooperative forms of all sizes as long as the self-monitoring aspect is maintained. Large groups must practice self-monitoring, although it may seem rather unwieldy.

I cannot give a definitive form for a cooperative group. But I can point out the process I use and let you create the form.

90. COOPERATIVE GROUP PROCESS

Form a cooperative group. Decide (as a group) what job or enjoyable experience you wish to do. Decide who will do or be or experience what. Decide whether you will trade tasks and, if so, how often. Decide how you will know if you are successful at this job or enjoyable experience. Do your job or experience. Decide how it went and what you would do the next time. Decide what you learned, what made you happy, and what made you unhappy about the experience. Now form another cooperative group and do another job or enjoyable experience.

COOPERATIVE LEARNING

The advantages of cooperative learning are enormous — ranging from children teaching each other and thus multiplying the number of teachers in a classroom, to responsibilities and efforts currently carried on in the classroom handled enthusiastically and responsibly by the students. Examples are:

1. Cooperation can lead to assisting every person in the classroom, including teachers. Ian loves to be a "handy helper" and he could be one every day if one of his jobs in the classroom was being cooperative, not just with the teacher but with the other children.

2. Cooperation can assist in multilevel learning, in which students learn skills and approaches that other students have and learn from the diverse backgrounds found in the classroom. If I am a visual learner and you are an auditory learner when we work together on a project I can develop my skills in learning in an auditory manner and you can develop yours for visual learning.

3. Cooperation teaches that most tasks can be done or information can be learned in a variety of ways, thus stimulating intellectual development and training children in flexibility and creativity in solving problems and doing work. If I thought there was only one way to learn to read by sounding out the words, but I learned your visual clues to remind me of certain words to speed up my capacity to learn, then I could adopt your technique. In the process I learn a skill that I could transfer to remembering names or other memorization processes. If I was having trouble understanding a math problem and you showed me how to solve it in a way different from the teacher or the book, then, rather than struggling I would use it.

4. The whole tenor of the classroom can change. If my classroom is made up of cliques that play together at recess and exclude others, this turns the playground into a battleground. Cooperation can make the classroom dynamic less traumatic and painful.

5. Learning accomplished together as part of a group task is more satisfying because the individual has the experience of inclusion, and of group success. I get to share my joys with others who are also finding joy and not resentment or jealousy in the moment.

In contemporary elementary and even secondary educations, most of the responsibility and control is in the hands of the teachers. Not only is this inefficient, but teachers cannot realistically take on all responsibilities and tasks of a classroom. Cooperation of children diminishes grade by grade, because cooperation is not a core concern. Children may not see the advantages of cooperation, and they rebel at the authority of adults. In many high schools, the amount of learning for the amount of time spent is limited and has diminished during the past several decades. Each of us gets to decide whether or not we want to continue this tradition.

Footnote:
(1.) Satir, Virginia; *The New Peoplemaking,* Science and Behavior Books, Inc., Mountain View, 1988, pp.194-207.

9. GOALS

Children are filled with all sorts of energy. It's a great natural resource. It is an untrammeled and abundantly available gift of life - whether positive cooperative and supportive acts, or in reaction, defiance and angry interaction with life. Training children to utilize a small portion of this energy in an ongoing manner is sufficient to put them firmly on the path to positive self-regard and success in life.

91. GUIDED PROCESS
FOR FULFILLMENT OF LIFE WORK

(With one person as the guide, say the following aloud to a group or individuals/children or adults.) The different stages can be done over a period of time or during a long session. Use conscious breathing and background music to relax participants before you start. *"You are walking and you come to a door. You look at the door, see what is is made of, what color, what size. You have the key in your hand and you unlock that door. On the other side it opens into the most wonderful place you have every visited - a place you see in your dreams. Before you is a path or walkway. You start along it. Before very long you see yourself as a small child. You see your face, your eyes, your hair, your expression as a small child. You stop and the child and you greet each other with love. You see all of the exuberance, joy, and hopefulness in this small child. You see that everything is possible for the small child you are or have been. You talk to this child. This child tells you very important things about yourself. This child knows that everything is possible."* (Continue this process adding further ages, depending upon the ages of the participants and their needs. At each stage, pause and allow the two to communicate. The younger/older version has important things to say to the individual in the process.) —

(CONTINUED ON NEXT PAGE)

The infant knows many important things about how life feels and about the greatness of the universe.

The pre-adolescent can see that you are a good actor and doer, and that you are having a great time in life.

The adolescent: can feel your power and vitality, a sense of life flowing through you without cease.

The early adult can feel the world about you in all its excitement and energy, a world to explore and know.

The middle-early adult experiences that you are an important part of the world you live in; you feel connected; you sense the part you play.

The established adult feels wonder in the universe and where you stand in it. You feel wonder at the variety and possibilities of others who exist in this universe with you.

The middle-aged adult feels humble and proud of your sense of vitality and life. You sense that you know much, more than you thought possible.

The senior knows you are all possibilities in but the smallest of actions or experiences. You savor life and the energy and vitality around you.

Conclusion: *"You have traveled far this day in this very special place. You feel very complete and good about all the meetings that you have had with the special person that you are. You return to the door. You pass through it, close, and lock it to return again another day."*

In order to go forward with our goals, it is important for each of us - adult and child - to see past periods of our life as complete and whole within themselves. We can see that we did what we were to do to the best of our ability in the past, given what we knew of ourselves and the world. Then we can let go of the past and go forward into our lives without the dead weight of past incompletions and sense of failure hanging onto us. Success has 4 billion different forms. This process can help each partici-pant come to appreciate his life work and experience as rich and fulfilling. The more often you do it, leaving pauses for different ages to talk to one another, the more old business can be finished, releasing energy for now. Use it in tandem with other guided exercises (eg., Secret Inner Talk with Yourself, #36, P. 70; Conscious Day Dreaming Exercise, #95 P. 161), in which the participants see themselves in the future and know that they have everything necessary to do their life tasks.

GOAL SETTING

Each of us has an infinite number of goals, children as well as adults. Often teachers and parents set goals for children. Too often this occurs without the child's participation or understanding of these goals. Adults want to do what is right for children and don't understand why children rebel or undermine adult goal projections for them. They also do not understand children's irresponsibility in the face of life tasks given to them. Certainly adults have many experiences of things they feel they must do but do not want to do. These have been traditionally called "responsibilities" or "obligations." Yet we often do these "responsibilities" because, as children, we were also told that we "must." Out of this experience, we adults think it is OK to insist that children do things that others tell them to do. Often this becomes the only experience that children have, that of being forced into obligations because our parents or adults had been forced into the same obligations. Goals that are freely and individually choosen or accepted will be given a child's full energy and commitment. Like adults, children forced or coerced into a wide variety of goals will eventually find ways of not achieving such goals. Furthermore, they may, in the process, cease to believe in their ability to pursue and achieve goals.

Goal processes put children in charge of their own life decisions. They become responsible to themselves. Responsibility then has a whole different meaning because they — and not some exterior adult "should" — are the source of their lives. They can learn to generate their own goals and the way to achieve them rather than rejecting or accepting demanded goals. Exterior goals, such as succeeding in school, can become their own interior goals as part of a long-term life plan.

Children are told to wait until they grow up so that they can decide what they will and will not do. But when they grow up, they still have not developed the processes to help them do the things they want to do, or realize the goals that they can conceive for themselves. Why wait until children are grown to teach goal-setting and goal-realizing processes? They can learn them even before they learn to read or write.

92. GOAL PROCESS

1. State your goals. Young children and even older children or adults can draw pictures of goals. Visual goals are often helpful for us to see ourselves achieving the things that we want.

2. Reformulate goals often. For example, read/see them daily. Rewrite/redraw them every few weeks. Do not be afraid to change any goal. If a goal is truly important to you, it will come back.

3. Prioritize your goals. Decide which ones you want to do now and which ones you want to do later.

4. Take action toward your goal whenever you can. Take small steps frequently.

5. Create a support system to realize your goals.

6. See what it is about yourself that needs to change or what you need to learn in order to move forward. Learning how you block or prevent yourself from realizing your goals helps you to release the block and to make the process natural and easy. like breathing.

7. Service: Find ways to do good for others and to feel more goodwill toward others. Practice giving.

This Goal Process will help those who want to move from aimless or reactive responses to goals imposed by others or a driven goal compulsion to a life in which accomplishment and service are as natural as eating and drinking. In truth the goals that motivate us throughout life will be those that serve our own self-understanding and self-esteem best. This Goal Process will help those who use it to become more conscious about their own processes in pursuit of a worthwhile life. In addition, they can slowly learn to find fulfillment in their own life processes. Thus the journey becomes as important as its end. If we are eternally placing all of our hopes in the end of the journey and considering the process of getting there bothersome and a burden, we will live lives that bother and burden us. Goal Processes can show children the relationship between who they are as individuals and how their life work reveals itself and develops in integrity as they grow and change.

I will briefly explain how the various steps work.

ESTABLISHING GOALS

Steps 1-3: We tend to flit from one want to another without knowing what is necessary and what is momentary. Later in life we begin to have bad cases of the "what ifs," in which we imagine that our lives would have been better if we had married someone else, lived somewhere else, had a different career, etc. Thinking about and pondering goals persistently over a period of time will help us to see what we truly value and what is not really all that important or interesting to us. Intitial priorities may change radically over time. In the process, children like adults will come to settle on personally meaningful values and goals. The time needed for sorting through goals may be several months or a lifetime.

Goal work can be used for children of any age. Ask young children to paste pictures cut out of books or make drawings on a piece of paper, which can be hung in their room or put in their desk. Perhaps they want to go camping or get along with a sister or brother. Any problem solving situation can be rephrased as a goal. They can rearrange the pictures at will, by cutting the paper again, or putting on new pictures, drawing things into old pictures, etc. For instance a young child's goal might be to have more friends. Then the child can cut out or draw pictures of what he sees as friendships; he can cut or draw pictures of games he likes to play with other children. He may make pictures of how he likes to play with other children, pictures of children resolving fights, of loyalty, and of support, etc. When the child looks at pictures of how he wants his life to be, he brings it within the context of his own experience. If he can create enough pictorial information for himself, then he will have a wider range of possibilities and will begin to experience the images from the pictures coming into his life. This goal fulfillment may not look the same, but it will have many of the same feelings about it. Perhaps the child who wants a friend will learn new skills such as introducing children to each other or telling each common interests. He will find in time that he has more and more successs in having friends and then he will go on to a new goal, and so on.

The process works deep within a person's mind to release knowledge of different ways to make the goals happen. The mind is working on the total context, not just the outward appearance. Our minds are complex and vast and have capacities we cannot even imagine. My mental capablities allowed me to walk on fire. When we work regularly to motivate ourselves toward the goals and desires that come from deep within, the answers also come from deep within. These answers often bring with them our total personal commitment and energy. Such personal goals can be powerful enough to change the course of a whole nation, as was the case with Ghandi. Often when doing such processes we will suddenly find everything falling together as if it had all been arranged by someone who could organize the universe. Some call this luck.

Adults and teachers can see in Goal Processes a tool for empowering children to do work at home and work in the classroom. Goals Processes then become integrated with normal everyday tasks. For instance, getting a bike may be connected with working to earn extra money. Or perhaps a child wants to be able to do art projects, and he begins to see how he can do art projects in his various other subjects in school. Thus he learns other subjects, and art becomes connected, rather than disconnected.

STEPS TOWARD GOALS

Step 4: Life unfolds moment by moment. Work on life tasks involves the totality of our lives. Taking small steps helps people make their self-learning and pursuit of goals and survival needs a normal part of life. We develop blocks when we think that in order to pursue some special goal, such as being a doctor or movie star, we must become extraordinary people. We may doubt that we can become such brilliant individuals. Yet if we start taking the small steps and turn our attention away from our imagined inadequacy the goal often arrives more quickly than we thought possible. Sometimes steps seem to move us away from our goal rather than toward it. This is not necessarily as it appears, for we may be doing steps important to our personal development in order to become the person able to do future steps. Many people who have successes are unable to continue them because they have not developed the character or inner strength necessary to continue this way of living and doing things. However, if goals are achieved in one's own rhythm - learning from the steps that seem to go backward as well as those that go forward - then success is more likely to be sustained.

SUPPORT FOR YOUR GOALS

Step 5: Initially it may seem that we do not need anyone else when we go about the process of goal setting and goal work. When we start taking small steps we quickly see that many people are involved even in our first tentative steps. A support system that networks, nutures, and sustains us in life and goal work helps integrate this as a ondinary part of life. Goal work then becomes like all problem-solving and relationship-healing work. It is important to keep goals from being secret dreams in the sense that in the secrecy of our hopes and expectations we tend to build up fantasies about how wonderful things will be once the goal has been attained. The greater the burden for magically solving all of life's problems, the more impossible a goal's realization can become.

As we develop our network at the beginning of goal work, we may feel very vulnerable and insecure. We need to trust ourselves and go slowly. We should share our goals only with people who care about us and would support whatever we do with our life. As we become confident with our support network, we can create broader Master Mind groups to support each other. A Master Mind group meets regularly to share goal processes. Each person supports the work of the others in the group through encouragement and by helping the other to see himself as successful and capable. Master Mind work refrains from advising or managing each other's goals.

A child's support network is often the family. However, children can also develop supportive relationships with classmates and friends as well as other trusted adults. To avoid classroom peer pressure forming and unforming support groups may be monitored by adults to ensure that each individual's goal aspirations are honored. Some children may prefer not to be in a support group at times or for long periods of time. If this is so, the teacher can find other ways to assist the child in continuing the process.

INDIVIDUALISM AND SUPPORT

Because we often imagine that doing some things must be incredibly difficult, we have a hording mentality toward our processes and their results, and therefore do not want to share them with others. We also have a tendency to believe that the results we create, the things we do, are a result of ourselves and ourselves alone. Thus we can feel very alone in what we do and wish to keep all of the failures and successes to ourselves. In time a person who does this process will come to realize that only beneficial goals can be shared and can be nurtured over long periods of time. This does not mean that we cannot do things that only we as individuals can do. Highly individualized goals can also be supported by a group. Yet, they work best in the context of other personal goals that can involve others and contribute to human society. We may also notice that the achievement of goals bringing good to others are the ones that last and also bring us the greatest sense of fulfillment.

Before we come to recognize the power of support, we are often involved in "using relationships" with other people. When one uses other people, she cannot be sure of their continued participation. Everything is very tentative. When one uses people, one's sense of self-worth is limited by the sort of ways that others can use her. This makes self-esteem a very tentative and temporary thing. In a sense, this is not self-esteem but simply a moment in which one's feelings of importance temporarily outweigh feelings of unimportance.

Often perfectly ordinary, but necessary, steps toward assuring basic survival become obvious and simple outgrowths of the goal processes that involve support groups. We learn that people will help us secure our basic survival needs. Often people who see themselves as very much alone will even neglect basic survival needs. Working with support networks slowly breaks down a sense of isolation. Even those with very rich lives can gain from greater depths of intimacy that support networks bring. Parts of and entire goals become inevitable outcomes as we create a supportive world about us. In developing support groups, we learn that they support us to the degree that we support them. If we wish such support to have few conditions then we must place few conditions on the support we give.

INNER CHANGES

Step 6: What do I need to change about myself? As our sense of our personal self-esteem grows and develops it opens a way for success to happen in our lives. This step is about becoming more loving and compassionate toward ourselves and others. We do not make big changes all at once but like this process, we make tiny adjustments continually. Often our fears impede our progress in achieving fulfillment. When we see ourselves in harmony with life goals, then achievement and success just naturally happen.

---

93. LOVING YOUR GOAL INTO EXISTENCE

Close your eyes. See how it is that you look, feel, and experience in relationship to this goal. Is there something about what you feel or experience about the goal that doesn't feel good? Are there deep fears and anxieties? Change it around in your mind or imagination until it feels happy, kind, or loving. Maybe you have to find another way of doing some things or being with others so that it will feel peaceful, comfortable, and happy to be pursuing your goal. See yourself changing things around. Try out all sorts of combinations of how you are when you are working toward your goals. Change a mad thought about someone to a glad thought. See yourself realizing the goal. See yourself as happy and totally loving. See your support and your process as joyous and fulfilling.

When we feel disconnected from what we want, and when we feel it is too hard or too distant, we seem to want to force it to occur, to "make" it happen. When we do so, we often do not feel like we are in control of our lives but must struggle for everything we get. This leads to stress and stress-related diseases. Ask yourself what you need to let go of - what fear, and what ambivalence about your ability blocks you? It is important to learn to release fear, anger, hostility and any desire that others be unhappy or unfortunate. The mind has learned to compulsively think negative things. We cannot reserve this negativity for others alone, so much of it also fall upon our thoughts about ourselves. We may think that someone else only cares about their own success, but secretly wonder if this isn't also true of ourselves. Become conscious each time you react to someone or wish to attack. Releasing attack thoughts and focusing upon good will magically (or so it seems) draw people toward you who wish you good in return. Like the infant who attracts love naturally, you will also attract support, assistance, and everything necessary to move your goal forward in a positive direction. Maurice Sendak's character, "Max" (*Where the Wild Things Are*) tells children how to relate to their fears (1.). Party with the monsters who say "no" to your dreams and you will be the hero of your own dreams.

SERVICE

Step 7: The more we contribute to life, the more life contributes to us. Learning to give is part of learning to receive. Learning to receive is part of success. You may believe that people with much money are good at receiving, but, unless they are constantly giving, their lives will be profoundly impoverished. Many seek only material wealth, believing that it frees them from all needs only to discover that they are no more happy with much money than they were with little. Some even feel that their earlier, poorer days were freer and happier. Generous giving of ourselves is a sign that we feel supported. Our goals come easily and effortlessly when we begin to reach the point where giving and service have become very important, expanding parts of our lives.

Children naturally and spontaneously want to give to others. They are taught to withhold, to give only conditionally. Supporting a child's natural desire to give and to give service to others is another way of supporting one of the inherent aspects of their sense of self-esteem. Service becomes more valuable in working with goals as it moves us toward the experience of freely giving without expecting anything in return. Ironically, when we do this we draw people toward us, because they like to be around giving people. Those drawn to us will inevitably include people who wish to support our goals.

CHILDREN AND GOALS

It is important that adults do not tell children which goals to have, which goals are good or better or more desirable, and which goals are less desirable. The children will discover these differences for themselves if they are allowed to monitor their own processes. There are many school/life-oriented lessons children will learn from a goal process: 1. They will learn that they can have their own goals and be in control of them as much as possible at all times. 2. They will learn that they can have goals that are personally meaningful to them. 3. They will learn that their commitment to their own goals can vary, and that many things that they thought were goals can cease to be goals or important after a while. 4. They will learn that that commitment often is related to how meaningful the goals are for them. 5. They will learn that realizing the goals involves commitment and an ongoing process. At times during this process the goals may seem impossible to obtain. 6. They will see that the realization of the goals involves all sorts of learning on their part - learning about themselves, learning about others, and learning about the world. They will often see how meaningful various tasks are. How much better for them to learn this lesson early and for themselves. 7. They will learn that some goals are easily accomplished and others are not, and that some goals are easily accomplished for some people but not for others. And visa versa. 8. They will find a relationship between their goals, their progress toward the goals, and what is going on within themselves. They will learn that they are in charge of their own destiny.

ADULT INVOLVEMENT
WITH A CHILD'S GOAL PROCESSES

In order to utilize goal setting with children, adults must learn many new skills in dealing with children. Adults need to learn new levels of trust and non-interference with a child's own processes and desires to interact with life and make positive contributions. Adults can create settings to support goal work and a self-determined approach to learning. This process is not all that different from the processes through which adults have learned to support a child's learning to talk and walk. In those learning situations, adults are far more passive and non-directive than they are even in the early years of education.

Modern education practices may interfer with goal setting, because teachers tend to take over all parts of a child's processes, from setting the goals, to determining the ways children will learn, to evaluating the outcome of goal processes. Education thus undermines many of the factors that empower children in their own self-determined process of learning. We have trusted children to learn to walk and talk. We need to learn to do so when it comes to learning to read, write, spell, and do math. Children learn from each other when learning to walk and talk. They also learn while playing. They learn to support one another while playing together. In supporting each other, children are learning important social skills, skills as necessary in post-industrial communications and high-tech businesses as are reading and writing.

GOAL SETTING IN THE CLASSROOM

This process can be used long-term in a classroom. You may find children will want to include classwork. As a child's confidence in his own processes grows, he will gain mastery over all aspects of tasks in his life. Even if never included, classwork will be deeply affected by goal processes. Children may automatically apply the principles to everything they do as they see that the principles work. The more distant children or adults are from the goal-setting process, the less connected they feel. It is my observation that children slowly disown the goals of the school system and rebel against them. They see the school's goals and their own as very separate. They often come to see the school's goals as self-serving, having little to do with their unique life. When children see their lives as separate from one of their primary social connections, schools, this can lead to problems for both. We see it in gangs, vandalism, and many antisocial acts. When children learn to utilize goal-setting and goal processes, they can become involved in the goals of schools. For they see the connection. This will be a boon to education.

94. A CONSCIOUS DAY DREAMING EXERCISE

(Adults or teachers may make this a guided process for the children or for other adults.) Close your eyes. Imagine the life that you want to live. See yourself in great detail. See the sorts of people you are interacting with. What are you doing with or for them? What are you giving to each other? What are they doing with or for you? Imagine the setting. What does it look like? What does it feel like? Imagine your life work? What does it look like? What does it feel like? How do you feel about yourself? How do you feel about where you are and your accomplishments? How do you feel about the people you interact with? Now open your eyes. Draw or write about what you have seen inside of you. Draw/write it so that it will help you remember what was best about this vision of yourself. What was it about you that you loved the best? Hang the drawing/writing somewhere so that you can see it every day.

When you do a guided process, take time for yourself or the participants to form images for each part of the process. Take time to experience and feel the emotions that come up during the process.

VISION AND GOALS

Even when you seem to have left behind the idealism of youth, it is possible to bring vitality and a sense of inner purpose to vocations and lives that have lost it. Individuals can experience burnout when they loose their vision. Adults who are not enthusaistic about giving to life feel that their efforts are making little difference in terms of what they originally envisioned. If they can change the focus from what they expect to have happen, as a result of their efforts, to how it feels to be of service to their own vision, they can bring back lost vitality and enthusiasm.

SERVICE AND VISION

My oldest grandchild, Nikki, came to me as he entered the second grade and told me when he grew up he was going to take care of trees and wild animals. I hope to honor the source of that aspiration within his highest self. this ability to generate visions for his life will keep him enthusiastic about life and loving what he is doing. Each child has the desire to make a positive contribution to life. That desire is our strength and our sustainer. When we stray from this inner purpose, we frequently go on to lead lives that are dissatisfying and, to us, meaningless. It is possible to see our lives as incredible gifts. When we do this we see that other people's lives are also gifts of inestimable value. Out of this realization comes a desire to be of service — to use this life for the good of all.

Being of service does not mean being a martyr or patsy or abandoning one's own life for that of others. Being of service ultimately means seeing one's work and one's involvement with life as more than a response to one's own needs. We do this when we form families and interact with children and spouses. If we stop at the borders of our family, then it can become a kingdom within a hostile territory. Service takes us beyond the limit of our known world. It allows us to transform the meaning of any task, no matter how negligible, from one that is self-serving, having only to do with our survival and our life, to work that is beneficial to all of humanity. In this transformation we learn to grow in our relationships with other people. We learn to care about others and their lives. This brings about a step ladder reciprocity; the more we care about others, the more we come to care about ourselves. And the more we come to care about ourselves, the more we care about others.

95. A SERVICE EXERCISE

Think of what you feel best doing - your work, your play, the ways you meet and interact with people. See how this work would contribute to your vision, the kind of world you want to live in. Imagine a life in which you follow your vision and you do what you like to do best and what you do best. See how the perfect world comes out of your service to your own potential and to the potential in others. Find a way to keep your vision before your mind's eye, even when you feel discouraged, or your vision doesn't seem to be possible.

There are countless ways that children and adults can be involved in service. As much as possible, allow them to make the choice. The more direct the service, the greater the value to the world and those who do serve.

1. Visit senior citizens homes.

2. Do work for ecological groups, such as the Nature Conservancy, or care for local parks.

3. Work for community groups - they vary from children's services to rape crisis intervention.

4. Older children can help younger children to learn in the schools.

5. Join 4-H or Boy or Girl Scouts. Many troups have public service units.

6. Adults can join Big Brother or Big Sister programs to work with children who need help.

7. Find a way to make your home or community more beautiful with flowers, murals, or other projects.

8. Adults who have businesses can give some time and energy to utilize their business skills to help people who need support in developing businesses or finding work.

9. One's own work and career experience can be the source of support for individuals struggling to bring that part of their lives together. Often simple support from the knowledge that anyone can make it, is all that it takes.

10. Be of service whenever you get the chance.

11. _____

Add your list of services.

PASSAGES

In my experience, life is like moving through doors. Once we have passed through another door our perspective, and even our experiences and relationships are complete in certain ways. When I first discovered this, I wanted to go back into the past and make everything neat and presentable. With time I have come to realize that I can't tidy things up. Then I understood that I did not want to go back. My goals, particularly my long-range ones to support my children and grandchildren in living happy and fulfilling lives, seem to lead me through the doors. Sometimes short-term goals will help us complete a passage, a life process to establish our own identity. We might call this goal completing college or getting a career going. In order to make the shift from one level of perception to the next, move through another door, we need to heal aspects of our past. We need to learn not to see past mistakes as failure but rather as a necessary learning step. One means of forgiving ourselves for past mistakes is to go back in our imagination and rearrange our lives in a way that makes the past more understandable. This way our past becomes a bridge to now, supporting us in our current vision and our current aspiration. When we regret or want to adjust our past, we have a hard time letting go of it. Our goal work can be an integrating and expanding part of our life process. Each step through a door is like stepping out onto a higher plateau; - the air is purer, we can breathe better, and we understand and know ourselves and our world more intimately.

Footnote:

(1.) Sendak, Maurice; *Where the Wild Things Are;* 1963, Harper, New York, 1984.

CONCLUSION

PRACTICE

There is no secret to the process of maintaining and strengthening positive self-esteem. If an athlete has the goal of going to the Olympics or simply developing greater physical fitness, she or he works at it every day. Day by day, you can use these exercises or ones you develop yourself to nurture a healthy sense of self-worth. After a while the daily regime starts to have an effect. Skills are built and perfected. Talent and mental attitude fuse, and a sense of success/OKness emerges from a confusion of counterproductive attitudes. A sense of being successful at being oneself takes on a life of its own and energizes one's whole life. If a family decides upon the goal of supporting and nurturing a positive sense of self, then the whole family begins to feel the effects. Each member's personal experience of life, step by step, becomes more peaceful and joyous. A school that takes on this goal and embarks on a daily regime can begin to notice its effects as it works its way through every aspect of the institution.

However, the process of supporting self-esteem is not a regime to be imposed upon children by adults who already have it "together." It is not a subject to be taught from text books. To be taught with conviction self-esteem can be best communicated by people who have acknowledged the importance of self-esteem in their own lives. Those who have already invested much in nurturing a positive sense of self-worth will not argue with the necessity of continuing throughout life to work with their own self-esteem issues. They know that, like any valuable asset, deep and thorough self-knowledge is carefully cultivated. They also understand that one cannot impose on others what you do not have yourself.

Those who have not yet developed a daily routine may want the instant pill form — one seminar or workshop to turn around their self-image forever so that they never have to think of about it again. They may invest much money in such endeavors only to find that they still must create a personal esteem daily care and feeding program.

Exercises in this volume will help you design an ongoing program and stimulate you to find support groups or develop your own program for yourself and the children in your life. The exercises are not graded according to age level. There are few concepts in these exercises that children will not understand. When you start working on self-esteem and relationship issues you may be surprised by how much children do know, at a very early age.

You may adapt the guided processes to a story-telling format for children, elaborating on the descriptive aspects. Children will have very vivid experiences within guided processes. These vivid experiences may even become upsetting or frightening. This is not a reason to abandon such work. The fears are there. They have simply come up in a safe setting. When children become aware of their fears, they can learn mastery over them just as adults do.

TAKING THE LID OFF

I have found in doing some of these exercises with classes that the students were very enthusiastic. They loved to do them, wanted to do and learn more, and interact in this new way. When they could talk freely, they took full advantage of it. I also found that I was "taking the lid off." When we take the lid off a pot of boiling water, hot steam rises. Where free self-expression has been suppressed, where talking is controlled by adults, a lid has been put on. It is a lid on self-understanding, as well. When we take the lid off, it feels like things are getting out-of-control. That is probably why a lid has been held on so firmly, out of a fear of chaos and anarchy.

The exercises all have rules and guidelines. In essence, the exercises are artificial. The artificiality ensures freedom and an evenhandedness (fairness), which may be lost in ordinary interaction. We are each unconscious about many of the patterns we have learned in communication, in our bodies, and in our social groupings. The artificial structure of the exercises helps us see the patterns. We can then identify patterns that are destructive and unhealthy. Exercises take the lid off the forms that we and our children have learned. The enormous energy pent up by keeping the lid on is released. If we were kept in a box too small to stand up in, day in day out, and suddenly we were let out of that box or put into a larger box, we would run and jump up and down. We would stretch and strengthen atrophied muscles. We learn whole new ways of relating. Everything about relating becomes new, exciting and somewhat confusing.Give children ways of releasing energy, and we also can give them ways of utilizing that energy. Thus the chapters on cooperative interactions and goal setting can give direction to that energy. I suggest that children be encouraged toward service to each other and to the greater community. Putting a child's tremendous energy into service allows her to be an active and responsible part of life. She can participate along with her peers rather than becoming involved in a peer group that acts out against the community.

THE INTELLECTUAL LID

When we put all of our awareness into our concepts, beliefs, and points of view, we move away from our experiences. We often lose touch with what is going on in our bodies, in the world about us, in the minds and feelings of others, and in our own intuition. We focus upon the intellectual and often lose sight of other forms of awareness. We use a small portion of our intelligence and our mind when we only consider our current belief systems. Much of education trains us in cultural belief systems. These are challenged from time to time by information that dispels stereotypical myths. The fine arts and practical classes, such as agriculture, home economics, shop, physical education and so forth, take us into less abstract and intellectual activities and engage other mental processes. Still these practical classes are often taught conceptually and abstractly. In art, for instance, we might learn about styles and techniques as valuable tools. Yet we don't learn how we come to make the choices about what to draw and how to draw it. Learning about our emotional connections to our art is important; it is the "why" of our interest in art. Technical knowledge it is the "how" that helps an artist to progress. That is, while our technique may improve, without a personal relationship to art we cannot progress as artists nor commit ourselves to pursuing the craft. Rather than being meaningful to us, it becomes another chore. This is why we see a lot of interest in art in the early grades and waning interest as time goes on. For small children, it is an alternative to talking, where they have limited skills. Older children have not learned to develop art's capacity to communicate, and so art loses its value. Many would not worry about loss of interest in art, often considered educationally unimportant, but this process is common to all subjects.

How do our relationships work? How do we interact with the world? What about the thousands of feelings and experiences we individuals have each moment? These are not theoretical but actual events in our lives. Why must we ignore all of this information coming to us instant by instant and force it into very broad intellectual generalizations and superficial concepts? Why don't we look at it and study it as we do various beliefs about math, history, reading, and writing? What keeps us in a standardized body of information and away from the reality of our own lives? Perhaps we need to ask why we practice these deep forms of denial. If the time that children spend in school were short, this would not be important. But this active process of focusing away from what is going on with children goes on eight hours a day, five days a week.

Concentrating on beliefs and theories and so-called facts alone becomes an escape from the reality of experience. University Professors teach "theoretical" living. Teachers escape from life and its real problems to worksheets, textbooks, and theoretical lives. If we train children, in constant conceptualization, we train them to avoid dealing with their lives. Is it any surprise when they find themselves unable to cope? We have a tight intellectual lid that keeps us from seeing what is right here and right now. This amounts to cultural and human denial. This lid limits the nurturing of self-esteem. In a theoretical world, we all are wanting, imperfect, inadequate. In the real world, right here and right now, we are who we are. When we take this lid off, we allow children whole realms of exploration of the here and now.

RESISTANCE IS NORMAL

When we decide to do something different or look at things about ourselves that we fear to see, we experience resistance. When we ask children to do things differently, they may want to argue and disagree. We all like patterns. Change brings up our fear of being out-of-control, our fear of being in situations we do not recognize. Many adolescents automatically respond with, "no" when an adult makes a demand of them. "No" is a very protective stance. We don't always know our limits or how to take care of ourselves, so "no" gives us time to regroup and figure out what to do.

There will be resistance to each of these exercises and practices. It is part of the process of learning. When we understand that this resistance is not forever, that children or adults do want to learn essential lessons inherent in these exercises, we can allow this resistance and reaction to occur. If we don't fight it, it may not last long. The resistance may return over and over again. It will test our commitment to positive self-esteem. The resistance does not mean that the exercises do not work or are valueless. The resistance is part of why we have negative self-images. It is based in fear. Fear can destroy self-confidence. When we become stronger than the fear, its power over us diminishes. We can become stronger by keeping our goals clear, primarily the goal of nurturing positive self-regard in everyone.

The following story illustrates the resistance to self-esteem enhancing processes that teachers encounter, and the success that this particular principal had as a result of persistence. I was at a school election for a small alternative school recently. The principal wanted each candidate to give a little speech before the election commenced. As the various students talked about giving their speeches, they complained that this was a "dumb" idea. Standing up and speaking publically before their peers is probably one of the most terrifying things that adolescents might contemplate. The principal understood intuitively the value of this experience, and insisted it go forward in a fairly casual way. However the candidate for president had contracted laryngitis, and didn't come to school that day. The principal persisted and she delivered the speech over the telephone microphone. Thus she made a small step toward overcoming this fear of speaking in front of her classmates.

THE LESSONS IN THE EXERCISES

The exercises are placed in the various chapters to further the understanding explored in each chapter. For instance, silent exercises are involved when we look at how we experience silence, how our body feels, what goes on in our mind, and how we relate to the world beyond the sensory data of sound. The talking exercises not only involve saying things, but how we say them, how we feel when we say them, and how we feel when others talk and how that affects what we say. All of the chapters could have an infinite variety of exercises. But any of the key exercises such as the "Insight Process" offer a lifetime of exploration.

For over 10 years I have been doing a silent inspection of my body sensations on a regular basis through a meditation technique. Slowly this has opened up for me understandings of whole realms of experience that I would never have understood had I simply read books or talked about understanding my body sensations. There is no substitution for this sort of knowledge. Through the process of exploring body experiences, I have become sensitive to the messages my body gives me. My sensations tell me not just about illness, but signal what I deeply feel about a situation, and communicate intuitions about things that will or might happen. What I learned from my body sensations leads me to understand that there is no way we can know what another person knows or feel what another person feels. We really only know "for certain" what is going on within ourselves. We guess at everything else. People can tell us what they feel and experience. Yet, unless we have identical experiences, we can only draw on similar experiences in order to understand what they might be trying to communicate to us. I have also found that the more I study myself the better I became at letting others communicate to me about themselves. When I was a theoretical person, trying to be a "perfect American woman," I was always caught up in trying to justify myself and show others how perfect I was. Learning about myself has freed me and allowed me to value being myself.

REPEATING SIMPLE PROCESSES TO LEARN DEEPLY EXPERIENCED TRUTHS

The exercises may seem deceptively simple. But it is possible to do any of them repetitively and learn much about oneself each time. The eyes-closed exercises, when done in a relaxing atmosphere, will help bring up information from deep within the mind. The same parts of the mind that we call upon to power our pursuit of our goals. Sometimes this information is deeply repressed experiences and beliefs. Sometimes these can be upsetting and frightening. Remember that the upset and fear is always there doing its work within our lives, whether we bring it up or not. When we allow it to come up, it can actually become part of our conscious thoughts — where we can see how it has been running our lives. Sometimes these deeply repressed thoughts have sabotaged our efforts toward happiness and success for years, even at times for our whole lives. We should not experience shame in thoughts coming to the surface. They are only thoughts, and people can have all sorts of thoughts. When working with children we need to allow them the privacy to deal with their own thoughts in their own ways and in their own timing. If they wish assistance, they can let us know. We need not pry. Simply helping them bring thoughts up is assistance enough.

FEAR OF EYES-CLOSED PROCESSES
Many people are very fearful of eyes-closed processes that allow repressed thoughts to come to the surface. We need to acknowledge that they do and can fear that many deeply repressed thoughts of their own will come to the surface and betray them. Often these people have cherished beliefs in the correct ways of thinking or looking at oneself. In order to maintain these beliefs, they cannot allow "bad" thoughts to come up. Thus they may believe that any guided or eyes-closed process is an "evil" process, because it allows those "bad" thoughts to surface.

I realize that teachers who wish to utilize the eyes-closed process may have interactions with parents who consider these exercises to be a threat to religious beliefs. If these parents can be assisted in understanding the value of releasing anger, suffering, and depression then they may be willing to support the use of eyes-closed work.

SCIENTIFIC OBSERVATION
Certainly all of the observation exercises are the staple of scientific observation. To observe our lives is a gift of inestimable value. We can't change patterns until we know what they are. We can't strengthen what is right and healthy when we are confused between what is nurturing and what is hostile and painful.

Constant use of such an exercise format throughout education, throughout the growth and maturation process of children, will bring a more responsible population of adults full of personal integrity and a passion for life. There is no substitute for fully experiencing our own lives. Learning about life out of a book is not the same as observing ourselves and how we are. Theoretical people in books are emotionally and spiritually distant from us. They offer ways of seeing alternative experiences, but unless applied to the "now" nature of our own lives, they distract us from ourselves, into the conceptual frameworks of denial, fears, suffering, and pain.

REPETITION

While repetition may seem boring, it allows the varied and unique response of each individual to become clear to him or her. Repetition of process-oriented exercises over time helps us see the patterned nature of our behavior and of its source in our thoughts. Being aware of how we think and how our thoughts move, change, and have patterns makes us masters of our own lives. If we don't know how we work how can we know how anything else in the world works? The world is a product of and is connected in someway with our human existence. When we see our patterns, we notice similar patterning processes in society.

Children are never too young to teach forms of self-understanding. If you are constantly exploring yourself, then you are teaching by example. However in a world of formal education, there are also formal ways of doing this. The formal means of education gives us tools to use and ways of creating tools. Just as math gives us a tool to keep track of our money, self-observation techniques give us a tool to keep track of ourselves. Life doesn't just happen to us, it is a product of how we go about living and, ultimately, thinking about living.

SUMMARY OF THE GOALS OF THE CHAPTERS

The format of the book came to me between the second and third draft of the book. And when this happened, the whole fell into place. Chapter by chapter we recreate movement of our understanding from the center of our being to our interaction with the world.

PRAISE

Praise is simply a way of expressing love and support. Maximizing the expression of positive regard is important for strengthening self-esteem. Wouldn't it be great if we lived in a world where everyone's first impulse was to communicate what is right with life?

SILENCE

We underestimate the importance of silence to our minds and bodies in our noisy, active, information-filled world. Silence needs to be at the center of our lives. When each of us seeks and utilizes times of silence during our days, we will find our lives becoming more peaceful, calm, and harmonious. We will also find our bodies healing better, and continuing to do so into old age. Silence is necessary for a number of exercises. And doing even a bit of one exercise each day will help you carve out a few moments for silence with yourself. I don't mean silence in which you plan tomorrow, your next move, or your grocery list. This silence is often very uncomfortable because many of us feel we must "do" something, constantly, to justify our existence. Your whole purpose is simply to "be" during your periods of silence. The gift of the realization that we need only "be" is powerful. When we need do nothing but "be," we will see how our life is a gift. When we let our children know that they are a gift to life, we have given them the whole of self-esteem.

LISTENING

Listening, as many have said, is not just a passive activity, waiting for our turn to talk. Listening is a primary way to connect ourselves with others. When we listen well, we hear not only the words but also the world of feelings and thoughts from which those words emerged. When we listen, we absorb the other person into our being. Our being has great intelligence and capacity to respond in ways that are supportive and nurturing of the other person and ourselves. When we impatiently listen, waiting to jump in with our thoughts, we will not notice the complexity of our own understanding of what is going on with us or with other people. We cannot write like Shakespeare or think like Einstein unless we take the time to access all that is going on within us with each experience of interaction. At first, it may seem to take a while to pay attention to what we are hearing and feeling when we listen with all of our being, but with practice it will go more quickly. Conversations can become miracles. Children are often closer to this process than adults. Children have not built up the conditioned concepts and prejudices that so often interrupt or control the process of listening. Adults may need to learn much about listening before they can interact with children as equals. Without 360 degree listening, positive and effective communication is impaired. The exercises and processes in this chapter are examples of techniques to help deepen our listening skills and support the process of detaching from reactive and compulsive listening patterns.

TALKING
From the time that we first learn to talk, we use talking as our primary means of negotiating life. We want to express ourselves, tell others who we are and what we feel, want, desire, and enjoy. We use talking to tell of closeness to others and our feeling of distance. Perhaps there was a time when grunts and groans were all that we needed in order to survive. However, in utilizing the incredible subtlety of talking, we can learn about ourselves and others. The flow between us and others can empower us and others or it can disempower. It contains the potential for initiating the acting-out of power imbalance, of interrelational dysfunctionality, and of antisocial impulses. Or it can be the means for healing all of the problems of the world, large and small. When communication is not working, we need to learn new ways of communicating. When communication is working, we learn new ways of being us.

When children enter education with fairly positive self-images and leave with those images diminished, this suggests that much needs to be done to change the nature of communication between adults and evolving children. Adults, in the process of strengthening their own sense of self-worth, can also learn new ways of communication which counter the diminution of self-esteem.

PEACE
A peaceful family and a peaceful classroom is what most of us want. Being peaceful does not prevent us from having fun and being joyous all of the time. Children are high-spirited and full of energy. We don't want to suppress or try to control that wonderful ebullience and enthusiasm for we do so at great risk. If we try to thwart and control children's natural liveliness in an attempt have a contained and orderly environment, we can slowly squelch their zest for learning and exploring life. When children become turned off to life, and to exploration, which are the heart and soul of learning, their function in the classroom and in the maturation process shifts from one of contributor to one of alienation. The goal of peace creates a way for adults, with all of their concerns

and goals, to interact with children and other adults so that everyone's curiosity, enthusiasm, and love of life is well served.

COOPERATION

While families are much smaller, the classroom in American schools often has 20 to 30 students. Families and classrooms could not exist without cooperation but competition, so prevalent elsewhere in society, also enters their dynamic, eg., in sibling rivalry. Competition seems fused with the "ideal" of being an American. Competition has deep psychic roots in our worries about our individual right to survive, and to validation, especially in comparison to those who seem stronger or want to impinge upon our fulfillment of our needs and desires. Many contemporary thinkers and even a few business leaders are beginning to feel that cooperation has qualities to solve persistent social and economic problems. Learning to form cooperative groups offers children ways to interact with each other in order to support and nurture positive self-regard. Schools have institutionalized many competitive forms, such as grading, competitive sports, individualized study, and learning patterns, but few cooperative ones. This chapters offers some thoughts and a few exercises to forward the process of forming cooperative groups and group projects.

GOALS

We all pursue goals. Often our pursuit is unconscious. When we fail or things go awry, we experience terrible feelings of loss, inadequacy, and low sense of self-worth. But we can teach ourselves and our children healthy processes to foster self-knowledge as we move toward fulfillment of these goals. We need no longer become unconsciously obsessive and compulsive in pursuit of goals at great cost to ourselves and others. As self-knowledge grows we can learn to achieve and fulfill goals in harmony with our own processes, thereby honoring ourselves and our loved ones.

OTHER CHAPTERS

This is a beginning. Many other chapters could be added to a book to assist with self-esteem. It is my hope that all who utilize this will create their own program and personal approach. That process will serve you best if it responds to who you are as a unique and wonderful part of life on this planet.

APPENDIX

ADAPTATION OF EXERCISES FOR CHILDREN

The following exercises have been adapted for children and are in the order in which they appear in the book. These are guides for adaptation; as many different wordings can be given, depending on the group and the pupose. The adaptations are made in a general language level for children but simplification of wording for younger than 8 years and sophistication for older than 13 years may be helpful.

Very young children may have trouble with words like "notice," and "observe." It may be worth your while explaining to the children and helping them learn the words. Or use substitute strings of words along with the more difficult but specific words. When I do guided processes with younger children I have had to explain words like "path." For observation exercises with children, you can build a perspective by telling them that they are detectives/or scientists, looking for clues. Children love games, so all exercises that can be framed as games are much more exciting and intriguing for them.

In guided exercises, leave time between the various instructions for the participants to create the images and feel the feelings. These exercises can bring back children's memories. These memories are of experiences with powerful effects. Generally children will bring up only what they feel safe about in the created context. If they are able to deal with difficult matters, then they may come up. Otherwise, children may sense that it is not safe and will not bring up experiences too difficult to handle.

CHAPTER I: INTRODUCTION

Instruction may be longer for children than for adults. You may not need every example of possible observations a child could make; you may need more concrete examples. You may want to make two or three separate exercises out of one. In the following example, you may first have them notice what they do, whether they argue, withdraw, or defend and try to convince. Then in the second session, they can watch their feelings. The third time, they can see how their mind works when they disagree. Separate steps may be easier for small children to handle than such a complex process as self-observation.

1. SEEING HOW I AM
WHEN I TALK TO SOMEONE ELSE (p. 4)

See what happens when you talk to someone else. If they don't agree, what do you do? Do you try to explain how you meant it? Do you try get them not to disagree with you? Do you argue with them? How does your body feel when you argue? Does it feel tight somewhere? Does it feel shakey or tingly? What are your other feelings? Are you mad? Are you sad? Do you feel like crying sometimes? Do you feel scared? Do you feel upset because you can never get people to listen to you? Do you feel that other people never want to think like you or understand you? What does your thinking cause your mind to do? Does your mind try to think of other things? Does your mind decide not to listen to another person? Do you think "what a mean person that other person is?" Do you think that he or she doesn't like you because he or she doesn't think the same way that you do? Are there other things your mind wants you to do, like go away or hide from that person? Do you want others to always think like you? When do you want them to think like you? When don't you care if they think like you? Keep your self-observations to yourself. You can put it in your journal. It will help you to see how you are. Watch if you think the same thing over and over.

2. REMEMBER A QUIET PLACE (p. 9)

Close your eyes and get quiet. See what thoughts you have. See the happy thoughts. See the scarey thoughts. See the thoughts like a movie inside your head. See thoughts about long time ago. See your thoughts about things that have just happened. See thoughts about tommorrow. See your thoughts about now. Get even quieter. See how nice it feels to get even quieter. See how you don't get tight. See how you breathe easy. Remember that quiet. Whenever you get scared or tight, think about that quiet and see if it will come back.

When you compare these adapatations to the adult version, you will notice that there are things in the adult versions that you may want to bring to the child-adapted version. To adapt, make the language simpler and have each sentence have one simple thought, if possible. For older children the language can be more complex. I will not make adaptions for each age but simply create simple versions and hope that you can use the general idea to adapt for other needs.

3. WATCH OTHER KIDS AND GROWNUPS (p. 13)

Sometime, when you can, watch other kids. See how they play all of the time. See how they have a good time. See what happens when they get into fights. See what happens when things don't happen right for them. See what happens when they are getting along with each other. Now see adults. See what they do. See if they play and have a good time. See if they have fights. See what they do when stuff doesn't go right for them. See how they are when everything is OK.

4. WELCOME TO THE WORLD (p. 17)

Close your eyes and listen carefully. Each kid takes a turn talking. Say: "Welcome to the world." "I'm glad you came." "I'm glad you're a girl." ("I'm glad you're a boy.") "Everybody is glad you came." "The stars and planets are glad you came to this world." "You are perfect just the way you are." "You are loved." "Without you being here the world would not be complete." "You are one of a kind." "You have a very special life." "Your being here is important." "What you will do here in your life no one else can do."

CHAPTER 2: PRAISE

5. I'M GLAD (p. 21)

See what makes you glad. See how much in your life can make you glad and happy. Look at every bit of it. See how glad all of it makes you. Feel yourself being glad.

6. I LIKE HOW SOMEONE ELSE IS (p. 23)

When I see someone else do something good I say so. When I see something that makes me happy I tell that person. I feel good when I get to tell others that they did something good. I like to say good things to other kids all the time. I like to see them happy. I like to see them smile. Even if I am not so happy myself, sometimes I can say something good to someone else. Sometimes this helps me feel better. Sometimes it doesn't. It is OK to say nice stuff to people all of the time. Now find someone near you. Tell them something nice, happy, or glad. Tell them a way that you like them. Tell them ways that you like what they do.

7. I LET THE GOOD IN (p. 24)

Close your eyes. Remember when someone said something nice to you. Remember when you were happy. Remember when someone loved you a lot. Remember how if felt. Remember what was happening then. What did you see? What did you hear and smell when you felt so good? Remember when a friend or someone in your family did something good for you or said something good to you. Remember how it felt. Look at that person and say inside your mind, "Thanks — I am so glad you did that and I am so glad to feel this inside of me when you are good to me." See how that person looks. What does his or her face look like? What is that person saying to you, now? Now inside your mind, tell yourself, "I am a great person. It's OK to be nice to other people." See how you feel about saying this to yourself. Say it again until you feel all warm inside.

8. SAYING SOMETHING GOOD
TO ANOTHER PERSON (p. 25)

See how you feel when you say something nice to another person. Are you embarrassed? Do you feel bad or ashamed?

Do you feel happy? Do you feel fuzzy and warm? Do you feel lots of different feelings? Do you sometimes feel good and sometimes feel not so great when you say something nice? Are there some people you can say nice things to and others that you cannot?

CHAPTER 3: EXERCISES

9. INSIDE AND OUTSIDE (p. 29)

Close your eyes. What is going on inside of you? What are your thinking? What does your body feel? What do your emotions feel? Open your eyes. What is outside of you? What does the world look like? What does it feel and smell like? What do you see that is important? What do you see that isn't important to you? See how people are. See how people are when they talk to you. Close your eyes. Remember what you saw. How does what you saw feel inside of you? How does your mind think about what you saw? Does your mind like to do this? What does it think about inside and outside?

10. JUST WATCHING MY BREATHING (p. 30)

Just watch your breathing. Pay attention when you breathe in. Pay attention when you breathe out. See how you have all kinds of thoughts when you are breathing. Try to feel the breathing. Let the thinking go by. If you can't feel the breathing, then breathe harder. See how quiet and rested you feel when you do this for a while.

11. MAKE YOUR OWN EXERCISE (p. 38)

Make up an exercise to do some work. Make up an exercise to have some fun. Make up the rules. Make up what you want to have happen. Decide how you want to have people be around each other. Talk about what you want to learn from your exercise. When you have finished your exercise, talk about whether you had a good time and learned something.

CHAPTER 4:
NONVERBAL COMMUNICATION

12. YOUR ATTENTION (p. 40)

Sit in a quite place, sometimes inside, sometimes outside. Watch everything. Watch your breath. See how you feel inside you. See what your thoughts are. Feel stuff around you — the wind, the sun, and even stuff you can't see at all. See everything around you. See close. See far away. Hear everything around you. Hear quiet. Hear loud. Hear it all. See if you can be aware of the tiniest things, sounds, smells, thoughts. See how tiny this stuff can get. Watch how you think about everything you are seeing, hearing, and feeling. See how you feel about it all. Do your feelings change. Do your thoughts change? Does the stuff around you change? See if you can notice tiny changes in your thoughts, in your feelings, in the world around you?

We can choose to use the above exercise to help children toward subtlety in awareness. Noticing very small differences is an important observation power. It can also be used to show how the mind tends to take us away from the here and now. This is another kind of subtlety. You could say: "See how when you think about thoughts, you don't hear sounds as well."

13. FEEL EVERYTHING IN YOUR BODY (p. 43)

Close your eyes. Feel your breath. Become quiet and peaceful. Feel the feelings around your nose. Feel whatever feeling you have around your nose. It could be tickly. It could be itchy. It could be cold, hot, or wiggly. It could be stabbing, painful, smooth, or nice. It could be any feeling. Feel the feelings on top of your head. These are called sensations. Feel the sensations, or body feelings, all over your head. Feel the sensations on your neck and your arm. Feel the sensations on your chest, your back, your stomach, your back side, and your bottom. Feel the sensations on your legs, and your feet. Go up and down your body feeling your sensations. See if you have any different thoughts when you are feeling your body sensations. See if you want to go to sleep, become antsy, or want to get up and get away. See how you feel when you have done this for a while. See if you feel more quiet and rested. See if your body feels good or relaxed.

13. Potentially this can be a very long exercise. You may want to break it up in parts and do a small part for a few minutes each day.

14. MY BODY IS SMART (p. 45)

Notice your body sensations. Notice that your body sensations change. Check out your body sensations when you are doing the stuff you do. Pay attention to your body sensations all day long. Now see if they change when you get scared. See if they change when you are happy. See if they change when you are angry. See if your body sensations change when you are excited. See if your body feelings change when something is about to happen. See if they change when something is about to happen and you don't know about it yet.

15. I AM PART OF THE WHOLE UNIVERSE (p. 46)

Go outside. You can do this at night. Imagine you are part of the whole huge universe. See yourself going by the stars. See yourself whizzing by the moon. Say, "Hi!" Now go back to the beginning of time. See the whole universe start up. Now go into the future billions of years. See the universe being there. See you can be everywhere in the universe. See how you feel when you do this. How does your body feel? See if you feel that it is OK to be part of the universe. If you do this again, notice how you feel the second time, the third, etc.

16. CUDDLING (p. 47)

When it feels safe cuddle. Cuddle with your parents and other family members. Even cuddle with brothers and sisters if it feels safe, or friends if that is safe. Get all warm and snuggly. Maybe read a nice storybook. Or just sit there. See how nice it feels. See if you feel if it is OK to cuddle.

18. TALK ABOUT TOUCHING (p. 49)

Talk about touching. What feels good? What is scary? What feels bad? Why do you like/need to be touched? How do you like to be touched? Can you say "don't touch me"? Can you say, "don't touch me like that"? Can you get people not to touch you in ways you don't like? Are there times when you are angry, sad, or hurt by how people touch you? Would you like to have people in your life who make sure that other people don't touch you in ways that you don't like? Can you talk with a person so that he/she can help you that way?

19. RULES FOR TOUCHING (p. 49)
Make up rules about touching. Make up rules at home. Make up rules at school. Say who can touch you and who can't. Say how much is OK and how much is not OK. Say what kind of touching is OK and what kind is not OK. Make up rules to make sure people who can hurt other people don't get to. Make up rules to make sure that everything is fair about touching. Make up rules so that you don't fight all the time about touching.

20. SEE HOW WE ARE ABOUT OUR BODIES (p. 50)
Be a detective. Go and watch people. See how they walk, run, and do things in their bodies. See if you can guess how they feel about their bodies. Do they like their bodies? Do their bodies feel good to them? Or do they feel uncomfortable in their bodies. See if you can guess from how they walk and move around what it's like to be in their body. Watch grownups and kids. See if their age makes a difference in how they feel about their bodies.

22. A JOURNAL ABOUT MY BODY (p. 54)
Be a scientist, a doctor, and a social observer. Make pictures or write what you notice about your body. Note the tiny things and the big things — the changes and the things that don't change. Note how you feel about different things and parts of your body. Note things that are interesting to you and things that are boring to you. Keep track of the changes. Maybe you can see how the changes affect you. Maybe you can see how changes are affecting other kids. Maybe you can see how bodies change. Maybe you can even see how there are tiny changes in the body all of the time. You can list all the stuff that is the same and all the stuff that is different. List changes. You can even list all of your thoughts about your body.

23. I LIKE MY BODY (p. 55)

Look at yourself in the mirror. Look at all the parts of your body. Say to yourself, "I like my head. I like my eyes. I like my hair," and so forth. Say it about all the parts of your body. Notice if you really do like those parts of your body. Even if you don't totally like them, say to yourself something nice about them. You will have this body all of your life.

24. I LIKE BODIES (p. 55)

Close your eyes. See yourself standing in front of yourself or see a member of your family, a friend, etc. In your mind say to yourself: "I am/This is a wonderful person. I have this is a great body. This is perfect for this person/for me. This is a whole and complete human being. I/he/she don't need to change a thing. My/his/her body is changing and evolving. It serves me well. It takes good care of me. I take good care of my body. I respect my/his/her body. I like all the fun things that my body can do. I have a fun body. I have a loving and supportive body.'

24. Varying this exercise, so that in their mind's eye they see parents, friends, handicapped, or exceptional people, minorities, etc. will help children and adults have tolerance for the wide range of bodies. This is particularly helpful as children approach adolescence.

25. BLIND MAN (p. 56)

Put on a blindfold or have a friend put on a blindfold. One of you lead the other around. Have them touch weird, nice, different, ordinary stuff. Have them hear strange, good, ordinary, or different sounds. Have them smell yucky, good, different, Ok smells. See how many different places you can walk, so that their feet and hands can feel all sorts of things and they can experience all sorts of things. Don't talk. Just move around. See how it feels to lead someone blindfolded. See how it feels to be blindfolded and have someone lead you around. Take turns. You can talk when you finish.

26. BODY TALK (p. 59)

Be a scientist and social watcher. See how people are different with their bodies. See if you can tell what they are trying to say with their bodies. See if they say things with their bodies rather than with talk. See if you can tell what the little things they do with their hands, head, feet, or torso mean to say. See if you talk with your body movements.

27. MIME (p. 61)

This is a game. Make teams. Use your hands, face, and whole body to show different things. Show feelings. Show ways people talk to each other without using their voices. Show things happening. Show characters. Show people you know. Pretend you are your parent, a teacher, principal, a famous person, or a character in a movie you like. Don't talk. See if the other team can guess who you are. Part 2. Make up a play or dance using these gestures without talking.

28. HOW MY BODY TALKS (p. 61)

Talk about what you see when you see people doing body talk. What do other people think they mean by their body talk. Do you see the same things? Do you see different things? Talk about why people use body talk. Tell others about how it feels to use body talk. When do you mime? Talk about what you learn when people do mime.

CHAPTER 5: LISTENING

29. LISTEN TO WHEN YOU WERE SMALLER (p. 62)

Close your eyes. See yourself when you were smaller. See your face. See your clothes. Smell the smells around you at this time. Feel how you were. Now listen. Hear the sounds. Hear people talking. Who is talking? Are you talking? What are people saying? If you are talking, what are you saying? Know that this has all happened a long time ago. It is OK. Give this smaller you some love. Feel yourself here in the place you are right now. Open your eyes.

29. Children are geniuses at knowing what to talk about and what to be quiet about. That is how they manage to take all sorts of horrifying experiences into adulthood without ever disclosing them. Sometimes the feelings they discover are painful, so it is important to have closure and tell them that they are loved right here and right now. This exercise can put children in touch with all the hearing that they did before they were able to speak. This exercise is only for teachers and parents who feel right about it. If it has the potential to place you in a position of worry or exposure, then do not use this exercise.

30. LISTEN TO OTHER KIDS (p. 63)

When you are on the playground or with other kids, just listen. Can you hear the different things they are saying? What are they saying about how they think about things? What are they saying about how they feel about themselves and other kids? What are they saying about the world around them? Listen hard and see if you can hear some of this, then watch how they move their bodies. Does it go along with the words?

30. Children and adults are intuitively and naturally observant. this observation exercise brings our ongoing perceptions to a more conscious level.

31. WHAT IS HAPPENING IN ME WHEN I HEAR OTHERS? (p. 64)

See what you are feeling when you hear other people. Do you feel happy, upset, sad, anxious, fearful, glad, peaceful? What are you thinking — a lot of thoughts, not many? Are you thinking that it is dumb, bad, smart, interesting? What is happening in your body? Do you get tight, an upset stomach, a light body, or any feeling? What do you think the other person is trying to say? What does it mean to him/her? What does it mean to you? Can you tell from your body what it means to you?

32. BE A MIRROR (p. 67)

Sit across from another kid. Take turns. One of you does what the other person does, just like a mirror. Then tell each other what it was like. How did it feel to be the mirror? How did you feel when the other kid was doing what you were doing?

33. BE A LISTENING MIRROR (p. 68)

In this game sit across from another person. When they say something, listen very hard. Then try to say back to them what they have said. Say it in your own words. See if you can get as close as possible to the meaning of what they said. When they are finished, have them tell you how it felt. Now you take your turn and have them be the listener and repeater.

34. BE A LISTENING MIRROR, #2 (p. 68)

Do the mirror listening game. This time become as much of a mirror as you can so that the other person talks a lot. Act as if you were interviewing him/her, except that you tell him/her what he/she said. See what the other person says. How much does that person say? If it is a shy kid, see if he/she can talk easily. See if that person feels OK about doing the game. When you are through, let him/her tell you what it felt like. Now take your turn.

35. HOW I FEEL WHEN SOMEONE IS LISTENING TO ME (p. 68)

Watch yourself. See what you feel when people seem to want to tell you what to do, how to think, what to be. Now notice what you feel when people just listen to you and tell you what you said, before they say what they want to say.

36. YOUR WONDER CHILD (p. 70)

Close your eyes. You are in your favorite place in the whole world. You are walking along. You hear the sounds of your favorite place. Maybe it is birds, the wind, or water. You feel the warmth or coolness of your favorite place all over your body and you feel nice inside. Someone comes to you. It is your Wonder Child. He/she smiles at you and is glad to see you. You laugh and play together. You feel free and OK. When you are through, your Wonder Child whispers something very important to you. You hear it and keep it in your heart. You say goodbye to your Wonder Child and walk some more in your favorite place. You come back so you can open your eyes.

37. LISTEN TO YOUR QUIETNESS (p. 71)

Close your eyes or keep them open as you wish. Listen to yourself. Listen to your thoughts. Listen to your body. Listen to your feelings. Now see if you can hear, feel, or experience quietness deep inside of you. See what it is like. See how long you can experience it. See what happens as you are experiencing it. Do your feelings interrupt? Does your body make a lot of noise? What happens? How does it feel to hear your quietness?

38. HEAR THE UNIVERSE (p. 71)

Be quiet and listen. Go past your thinking. Go past your body. Go past the sounds of the ouside. The cars, birds, or wind. Keep on going to the sounds of the universe. Even if you can't quite hear them, imagine what they are like. Listen and maybe you can hear a bit of the sun, moon, and space. Maybe you can hear the whole of the earth changing and being. Maybe you can hear all of the people on the planet. See if you can feel, sense, and hear it all.

38. Feeling and sensing are like hearing: they function partly in the realm of the invisible. As we become more consciously aware of ourselves, the subtlety of our awareness grows. This is a stretching exercise like you would do in an aerobics class. It helps us stretch our capacity to experience the world around us. Many children are aware of all sorts of things beyond the range of the senses that adults call "normal." We need to honor this awareness, even if it is part of a child's imaginary world. It plays a part in their unique life. Sensitivity to subtle experiences and feelings helps children take care of themselves and avoid accidents.

CHAPTER 6: TALKING

39. SHARING (p. 74)

Share yourself with others. Talk about who you are. Talk about what you like to do and what you don't like to do. Talk about your favorite people, your friends, and your family. Talk about your favorite animals. Talk about what makes you happy and what makes you sad. Talk about how you look. Talk about what you think are your good abilities. Talk about things you'd like to do. Talk about things you'd like to do better.

39. You can ask the children to draw pictures of important points in their lives on a long strip of paper. Then they can write captions, long or short, next to each illustrated scene.

40. INTERVIEWING (p. 75)

Interview someone. Ask them questions. You can ask questions that you've written down. You can ask questions about things you are interested in, like horses, work, sports, or anything. You can talk to them like you would anyone else and ask questions because you have decided you are going to interview that person. Practice interviewing. It is a good way to get to know things about the world that you don't already know.

41. PICTURE OF MYSELF (p. 76)

Draw yourself. Draw everything you can think of about yourself. Tell someone about your drawing of yourself like you were being interviewed on TV.

42. JOURNAL (p. 78)

Keep a journal. Write the date. Write about anything that you want to keep a record of — perhaps it is things that you want to do, or remember. You can write down stories. You can write down things about your life, friends, and family. Write down what happened at school or when you were doing fun things. From time to time go, back and read your journal; it will tell you what a good job you are doing at being you.

43. WRITING ABOUT MYSELF (p. 79)

Make a story about yourself. You can make a series of pictures, write it in words, or talk about it on a tape recorder or video. Tell what you like to do; talk or write about things that have happened in your life and about people in your life, and about animals, and toys, and places you have been. Talk or write about about things that are exciting, scary, interesting, or hard things to do. Write or talk about your whole life, when you were a baby, when you were growing up, about different times you think were important or special, and anything else.

44. MY LIFE STORY, PART II (p. 79)

Your story can be a big project. You can make many pictures, stories, and videos — talking about different times in your life and different things that have happened. You can have lots and lots of details. Maybe you can do this over the course of the school year and work on it a little bit every day. Or put parts together each week. You can look and see what you have. It can be like a journal, a series, or short stories about yourself. Maybe you can share it with your school, your parents, or anyone who would be interested in and happy about you and your life. Maybe you want to keep it to yourself.

45. HISTORY SPOKEN OUTLOUD (p. 81)

Make a history of your family. Talk to your grandparents, parents, aunts, uncles, cousins, sisters, brothers, or anyone else in your family. Make a record, like in a history book, of important things that have happened in your family — things people did, things that happened to people, sad things, and happy things. See the part your family played in how this country/society is.

46. TELEPHONE (p. 82)

Sit in a circle. One person starts. She whispers something into the ear of the person next to her, then that person whispers to the next person, and the next, until it has been whispered all around the circle. See if you can do this until the message comes back exactly as the first person said it.

47. SAYING AND NOT SAYING THINGS (p. 82)

Watch people talking. See if you can tell whether they are saying what they feel. If they are not saying what they are feeling, see if you can tell what they are feeling. Can you sense their feelings from how their voice sounds, from how they move or hold their body, or the kind of words they use such as angry words, sad words, happy words?

48. INTENTION (p. 83)

"Intention" is what people really want. When you watch people doing things or talking, see if you can guess or figure out what their intention is. Go ask them if you are right, if that feels OK to you. If it is not OK to ask them, continue to watch and maybe you will find out anyway.

49. DIFFERENT WAYS YOU CAN TALK (p. 83)

In this game pick out something to talk about. See how many ways you can say the same thing. See how many different feelings you can put on what you say. See how many different kinds of words and thoughts you can use to say just that one thing. Perhaps you can make up teams and see what team can make up the biggest number of different ways of saying the same thing.

50. I FEEL (p. 84)

Talk about yourself. Say, "I feel..." or "I think..." or "I believe..." Try to talk for a long time saying only what is true for you. See how it feels to say this for yourself. Let other children talk this way too. How does it feel to have everyone talk in "I" statements, speaking only for themselves.

51. WATCH YOURSELF SAYING YOUR FEELINGS (p. 84)

Watch yourself when you say what you feel, what you think, and what you believe. See if it is scary, if it is sad, if it makes you angry or happy. When you tell others who you are, see what happens. What happens with adults, or other children? Are they happy, sad, angry, etc.? Watch what you feel when others react to what you say.

52. A PROCESS TO STOP FIGHTING (p. 85)

Have two fighting or disagreeing kids talk to each other while other kids are facilitators. The fighting kids talk about why they are fighting. The facilitators listen. The facilitators ask the fighting kids to repeat their complaints. They ask questions about what happened and listen, but they don't take sides or decide who was right or wrong. The facilitators just let the fighting kids say everything that needs to be said. The fighting kids can't hit or touch each other. They just have to talk. The facilitators can help the fighting kids to listen to each other. When the fighting kids feel it is OK and have a solution, you stop. If they don't have an answer, they can do the process again at a planned time.

53. SAME AND DIFFERENT (p. 86)

Sit with a bunch of kids or adults. Talk about who is the same and different. How are you different? Are you different ages? Different sexes? Did you, your parents, or your great grandparents come from different parts of the world? Did they speak different languages, wear different clothes, or eat different food? Do you like different music, food, or toys? Tell each other every thing that is different. Now talk about how you are the same. See what is the same in each person. Do you live in the same area, speak the same language, hear the same news, go to the same school, live on the same planet, smell the same flowers, or have the same biological stuff in your body? Now talk about how same and different work together. Talk about whether they are important to one another. What makes same? What makes different?

54. WHO GETS TO HAVE THEIR SAY (p. 88)

Watch people talking. Who gets to have their say the most often? How does that person show that he/she thinks he/she is more important than the other person? Observe all the little parts that make it so that he/she gets to have her/his say — the way he/she uses hands, face, loud, or soft voice. What feeling is in the voice of the person who thinks he/she is most important? What feeling is in the voice of the person who thinks they are less important? Just notice this. You can share what you see with other people who are also noticing.

55. TALKING CIRCLE (INSIGHT PROCESS) (p. 90)

Take turns talking in a group. Each person gets to talk all by him/herself until he/she is done. Each person can say whatever he wants and as much as he wants. Try to make "I" statements. Make "I" statements especially when talking about other people. Everybody else listens. Try to listen carefully and hard. Everybody else should respect the person who talks. No put downs. No making noises meant to make that person feel bad. If that person says something that she/he does not want you to share outside of that talking circle, then you don't share it. Everybody tries to "honor" the other person's feelings. No arguing or talking back and forth. This is a one-person-at-a-time process. Try to do this process as often as possible so that you all get to say all that you need to say.

56. WATCHING ATTACK
AND DEFENSE TALKING (p. 93)

Watch when someone attacks with words. This means they say something that accuses another person or tells another that he/she is wrong, bad, or has made a mistake. Watch when someone tries to defend him/herself against an attack of words. What do they do? Do they try to explain? Do they attack in return? Do they change the subject? What do they seem to feel? What are you feeling when you watch this? Just notice and share what you see.

57. BOYS AND GIRLS (p. 96)

Make a talking circle. Talk about boys and girls. What do you think is different? What do you think is the same? How do boys and girls get along? How do they not get along? When you grow up, how do you think you will act as a boy/or girl? How do you expect the opposite sex to act when you grow up? How does your dad act? Your mom? How do other grown up men act? How do other grown up women act? Share what is safe. Try to share difficult or unpopular ideas about being a boy or girl.

57. Learning to share our feelings is not always a safe and empowering experience. Sharing just a bit at a time can teach a child to slowly liberate him/herself from the fear of peer or

*adult disapproval of his/her feelings. Feelings are not danger-
ous. All feelings are OK. We have problems with feelings, when
the feelings manifest as actions. When expressed and shared as
feelings, all can be vented and let go. Often children feel they
must hold down all of their feelings. Then they become like volcanoes ready to erupt.*

58. WHERE IT IS SAFE (p. 97)

Close your eyes. Imagine a place where it is totally safe to be
yourself. Imagine you can say whatever you want. Imagine
you can do what you need to do to take care of yourself and be
free and enjoy your life. Imagine that everyone knows who
you really are and likes you just that way. Imagine that you
know that most people really do love you and care that all
goes well in your life. Imagine that you can be part in creating
a world where it is safe to just be you.

59. TALK ABOUT MAKING IT SAFE (p. 98)

Make a talking circle. Talk about making it safe for everyone
to be themselves. Talk about what you would need to do to
make it safe. Talk about what other people would need to do.
Talk about what is scary when you think about making it safe.
Talk about keeping secrets and respecting each other. Talk
about why you would want to make it safe.

60. WHAT IF I WERE A BOY/GIRL? (p. 99)

Close your eyes. Imagine if you had been born a boy/girl
(black, Asian, or with a handicap). What would it feel like?
How would you speak differently? What clothes would you
wear? What games would you play? What friends would you
have? How would your friends talk to you and be with you? How
would your parents act toward you if you had been born the
other sex? How would other adults act toward you? What kind
of job do you think you would plan to get when you grew up?
What sort of fun could you have that you coudn't have if you
were someone else? What things could you do if born a different gender that you can't do because you are a boy/girl? Think
of all the details, especially what it might feel like.

61. DRAMA GAME (p. 102)

Make up teams. One person at a time on each team take turns acting. One point for an feeling — like mad, sad, happy, dispair, pain, etc. Two points for a role — like a farmer, a mother, a baby, a carpenter, a president, etc. Three points for a character — like Indiana Jones, President Lincoln, Janet Jackson, etc. The team with the most points wins.

62. DO A DIFFERENT ROLE (p. 103)

Role play with other kids. One of you can be the person who is mad or hurt, or any role in a situation that you want to understand. Then the other person does the other role. For example, one person is fighting with another person about who is right. Two kids can take the roles, then you can see how you act when you are fighting about who is right. You can try out new and different ways of acting. You can try out lots of different possibilities.

63. PLAY MAKING (p. 104)

Using role, dialogue, and interaction, make up a play. The roles become characters that you want to play. Put the characters together in a story. Get together as teams and each make up a script. Write it down or draw pictures of how you want to do your different roles or the story. Perhaps you can make up paper sets or move desks and furniture around to create sets. Then have each team present their play to the other teams or to the whole group.

64. DIFFERENT VOICES INSIDE OF MYSELF (p. 105)

Work in a safe space, with another person/kid in your group. Find a voice inside of yourself. First you will find the voice that has a say about all the voices inside of you. Let that voice talk. Then find the other voices inside of you. One voice could be a baby, a shy person, a mad person, a funny person, or an old wise person. Let that voice talk and say whatever it wants to say, then maybe another voice wants to talk. Let that voice talk. You can let the voices talk to the other kid or a person that you are working with. After a while talk to the voice that has a say over the other voices. Then let the other person have his turn. After doing this for a while, you can use what you learn to make your plays and your drama game.

65. TALK SHOW (p. 106)

This is a talk show game. One kid can be the host. Other kids can be the guests. Others can be the audience. You can talk about special things that the guests do or know. Maybe you can use it for school subjects, sports, movies, books, favorite toys, or games. Or you can discuss problems like ecology, or fighting at school. Maybe you want to videotape the talk show and look at it afterward. Play with it: try out all sorts of ways to be a talk show.

66. YOUR THEATER (p. 107)

Make up plays about your world or about problems you are having at school or home. Get together with other kids and make up the plays. Write down the words you are going to say. What are the best ways and who are the best characters to have say the things that need saying? What kind of stories do you want to tell? What are the best characters for the stories? Which kids should do the different characters? How will you get the actors to do a good job? How will you develop the characters so that they can make the story happen in a believable way? Maybe you want to look at other plays to see how other people have done this. Make up your play. Rehearse it; practice it until you feel good about it. Then put it on for other people to watch. When you are done maybe you can share how it was for you. Let everyone have a turn sharing in a Talking Circle. Then you can make up another play and use what you have learned.

66B. PLAYS FROM YOUR IMAGINATION (p. 107)

Create plays about people who are very different from you, about children with handicaps, about people from history or from different countries, or about people from the future or from imaginary places, like fairies and elves. Tell stories that you like, stories which are wonderful, exciting, adventurous, scary, or heroic. Then each person can have a turn being the good guy and being the bad guy, the beautiful fairy princess and the evil witch. Use everything you learned from your other drama exercises. Each exercise will help the others, and you will get better and better at it.

CHAPTER 7: PEACE

67. CHAMPION OF PEACE (p. 110)

Close your eyes. Imagine you are your favorite superhero or superheroine — Superman, Wonder Woman, or someone like that. The world is going to be destroyed. Volcanoes are blowing up, and tidal waves and hurricanes are coming to all kinds of places. There is no rainfall and all life is dying. War is breaking out and people are starving. Because you are a superhero, you are going to save the world. See the first thing you are going to do to save the world. See yourself do it. Take all the time you need. Now see the next thing you will do to save the world. See every detail of it. Now see the next thing. Now see how it feels to be in the world when the terrible things start to go away. Now look and see what a good job you have done to save the world.

67. Have children share with each other what took place in this inner process. They can write about it in journals or tell stories about themselves. They can also create plays, games, and school projects in response to what they experienced in this imaginary interaction with the world. Children do this kind of fantasy often. It is the fuel of each child's personal idealism.

69. BE AT PEACE (p. 111)

See if you feel peace. Check out inside of yourself. If you don't feel peace. See what you are feeling inside. Just see what your feelings are. See if the peace part is there underneath the other feelings, and find it; it's there all of the time. See if you can find your peace feelings somewhere inside, let them get strong.

70. PEACE CHAIR (p. 114)

Have a peace chair at home or in your classroom. You can go there when things are upsetting - when you feel bad or unhappy, or when you have a hard time with other kids, when adults are mad at you, or when you feel you have done things that are wrong or messed up. See if you can feel quiet and OK when you are in/on the peace chair. See if you can get to where you feel you can take care of what went wrong.

71. OBSERVE PUNISHMENT (p. 115)

Observe. What does it feel like when you are punished or controlled? What does it feel like for others to be punished or controlled? What does it feel like for you to watch others being punished or controlled? Do you punish or control other people? How do you punish or try to control others? How do you feel when you are punishing or trying to control someone else? Just observe or watch.

72. TALK ABOUT PUNISHMENT (p. 116)

Talk about being punished. What do you feel about it? Talk about what happens when something goes wrong or you do something wrong. Talk about doing what adults want you to do. Talk about control. Control is when people want everything to go their way or be in some sort of order. Talk about how it feels to have everything in some order. Talk about how you feel about other kids being punished.

73. PEACE AGREEMENT (p. 118)

Decide with grownups, teachers, or parents, what you each will do to see that there is peace amongst you all. Talk about how each of you will know that you are doing your part. Talk about what you will do when things go well, and what you will do when they don't. Talk about what you want this agreement to be about. Talk about how you want to be treated and how you want to treat others. What you want to do and have others do with and for you? Even talk about how you want to feel when you are part of this agreement. Talk about changing the agreement when you and the grown up feel it needs changing. How will you change it? Talk about how the agreement will help everyone who is part of it be at peace.

74. SEE HOW WE CONTROL EACH OTHER (p. 119)

Watch when people try to get someone else to do what they want them to do. See what happens. Is the person who wants the other person to do something bigger, stronger, smarter, older, or richer? Or is the person smaller, weaker, less educated, younger, or poorer? How do they try to talk the other into doing that thing? Does the other person seem to want to do that thing? If the other person does want to do it then what happens?

If the other person doesn't want to, then what happens? See what the person who wants them to do it does next? Does that person try to convince the other person? Does he/she bribe that person to do the thing? Does he threaten that person? Do they make an agreement? Just watch.

75. WHEN I FEEL I CAN'T DO AND FEEL WHAT I WANT TO (p. 120)

Observe when you feel you can't do or feel what you want to. Notice when that happens. See what other people are doing. See what you think they are doing that keeps you from doing what you want to. See what you are thinking when you can't do what you want to. What are you feeling and thinking about others who seem to keep you from doing what you want to?

76. SEEING IT DIFFERENTLY (p. 120)

Imagine a time when you couldn't do what you wanted to do. Remember how it felt — how frustrated, unhappy, or sad you felt. Now see if you can see what happened from another place, as if you were another person just watching what went on. See if you can see something you learned from not being able to do what you wanted to do. See if you can see that maybe you became smarter, stronger, or wiser out of what happened when you didn't get things just exactly how you wanted them.

75-76. I have divided this exercise into two parts so children can become clearly aware of both their feelings and the possibility of learning or growing through feelings.

77. RESPONSIBILITY (p. 121)

See if you can observe responsibility. Can you tell when people are responsible for what is happening with or to them? Can you tell when people don't want to be responsible for what is happening to and with them? Can you notice how you feel and act toward responsibility? Can you tell where one person's responsibility starts and another person's starts? Just observe. You will notice that this is not easy to tell. That's OK. Just noticing the difficulties is useful.

78. MAKING YOUR FORCE FIELD (p. 123)

In this game, imagine that you have a force field around you. Each child has a force field, and must be very very aware of the other child's force field. Each of you talk as if that force field was there. Maybe your force field makes a sound when people get too close. Maybe other children feel it a little bit. Imagine how safe it feels when you have the sheilds from your force field up. See how people have to come and ask if your force field is up before they can say things to you or touch you. What does that feel like? What does it feel like to have your own force field? How does it feel when other kids have a force field around them? You can talk about it when you are finished with the game.

CHAPTER 8: COOPERATION

79. COMPETITION AND COOPERATION (p. 127)

Watch children in competition. For instance. in sports, when one person wins a race. Watch when kids or adults do ordinary things in school, but one is the best. See how kids are talking to each other when there is competition. See how they walk around and act when there is competition. Now watch children in cooperation. Cooperation is when everyone does things together, and no one person is the best. For example, when everyone in your family makes dinner together or does the dishes, that's cooperation. In a disaster like a hurricane people cooperate and help each other out. See if you can see when kids at school, your family, parents, or teachers are cooperating. See how people talk when they cooperate. See how they act when they cooperate.

80. SEE COOPERATION AT HOME (p. 128)

When you are home, watch cooperation in your family. See what each person does to help the others get work done or have fun. See how your family acts when it is cooperating. See how you talk to one another when you are cooperating. How do you feel when your family is cooperating? What feels good? What doesn't feel so good?

82. IN YOUR COOPERATIVE WORLD (p. 129)

Close your eyes. You are in one of your favorite places. It is very beautiful — a nice day. You are here with your cooperative group. You look at all the people in your cooperative group. You look at their faces and their hands, and at what they are doing. You see them talking to you. You see yourself talking to each of them. You recognize their faces. You know their names. You know what they like and what they feel and think. You all play together and have fun. You work together. You eat together. Each person respects and cares about all the others. Each person has his own space and place to be. Each person has a way to live independently and take care of himself. It is very calm and peaceful but full of fun and joy. You are glad to be with these people and they are glad to be with you.

83. WHAT HAPPENS WHEN PEOPLE WANT TO BE BOSS? (p. 135)

Watch when you are in a group. Who wants to be boss? Do you want to be boss? Do you not want to be boss? How do people seem to feel when someone is boss? How do they act toward the boss? How do they act toward someone who is not the boss? What happens if more than one person tries to be the boss? Do you feel that some people should be boss and some people should not? How do you feel when there isn't any boss?

84. WANTING TO HAVE EVERYTHING MY WAY

Watch when you are with a group. Do you want to have everything your way? How does it feel when things don't get done your way? How does it feel when someone else in the group wants to have everything his/her way? How does it feel if one person gets to have most of the things done his/her way? See if the group can find different ways to have fun or get things done.

85. WHEN IS THERE COOPERATION? (p. 137)

When you are watching people cooperate see if you can tell when they are not being cooperative. See if you can tell when cooperation and competition get all mixed up. See if you can see when people decide to be "the boss." What happens to the people who are bossed? How do they act? How does the boss act in return? Watch to see if you can tell when people want to have more cooperation when they are doing something together. How do they have this happen? What does the shift back and forth between cooperation and competition feel like?

86. THE ROPE GAME (p. 138)

Put a rope around all the members of your group. Tie it so that each person is attached. (Make individual rope belts.) Each person takes turns pulling on the rope. See what happens when they do. Talk about how it feels when people pull on the rope. Talk about how it feels when you pull on the rope.

87. HOW AM I IN A GROUP? (p. 139)

Close your eyes. Remember how you are in a group. See what you do. See what you say and how you say it to the other people in the group. See how you feel. See what happens with bosses and getting to do things your way. See how you feel when people work and play with you in different ways. See how you feel if no one works or plays with you. Do certain people work and play with you and others don't? Do all people work and play with you equally in the group? See how you feel if you play and work with nobody, if you do it with just a few, or with all. Are there some people you like to work and play with and some you don't? See yourself working and playing with those you don't like to deal with.

88. HOW IS MY GROUP DOING?

Talk about how your group is doing. What makes you each happy? Unhappy? Uncomfortable? What is not going well? What makes it possible to do what you are doing? What makes it hard? When do you feel that you will accomplish what you are doing? When do you feel that you won't get it done? How would you change it? How would you keep it the same? What do you like about what you are doing in the group? What do you like about the group and what it is doing?

89. WHAT IS IMPORTANT? (p. 146)

Talk about: democracy, freedom, commitment, integrity, trust, responsibility, and success. What does each mean to you? What does each idea mean when you are working or playing with other people, kids? How important are each of these ideas of goals to you? (Adults, parents, teachers, define these terms when needed.)

90. MAKE A COOPERATIVE GROUP (p. 148)

Make a cooperative group. Decide amongst yourselves what you are going to do — what work and what fun. Decide how you will take care of people wanting to be bosses and wanting to do everything their own way. Decide how you will decide on things. Decide how you will know when you have done things well and when you have made mistakes. Decide how you will make sure that everyone is doing OK. Do something with your cooperative group, then talk about how it went. What went well and what didn't work well? Then decide on another project to do with your cooperative group, make changes in how you do your cooperative group, or create a new cooperative group.

CHAPTER 9: GOALS

91. MY LIFE IS SUCCESSFUL (p. 150-151)

Close your eyes. You are walking. You come to a door. You have the key and open it up. On the other side is a walkway through a beautiful place. You walk along and you see a person walking toward you. You see that it is you when you are an adult.(Vary ages, see process in text, p. 150.) You see your hair, your eyes, your face, your clothes, everything about you when you are an adult. Your adult self is smiling at you with great love and compassion. She/he is very happy to see you. You talk to each other. (Have silent pauses for all of the following.) He/she has important things to tell you. You have important things to tell him/her. If you want you can tell him/her about your worries about growing up, about your anxieties about what life will be like then. You can tell about your happy expectations and your great goals. He/she is excited about all your plans. You hug each other with joy and love. You feel very calm and joyous. You go back on the walkway to the door. You go through the door and lock it again as you leave. You are back in your world.

92. GOALS (p. 153)

Put down your goals. Make drawings, cut out pictures, or write them. Rearrange them anytime you want. Change them.

Replace them. Do whatever you feel you want to do, because they are your goals. Choose the most important few. Do small steps for each goal, if only to think about them every day. Find people who like you and want you to have your goals. Talk to them when you feel you need to about how you are doing. Let them talk to you about their goals, too. Be helpful to people whenever possible. Find ways in which you can be of help to this world, and do your helping work often. Try to get over angry and unhappy thoughts about people as soon as possible. Service and letting go of unhappy thoughts will help you move toward success with your goals.

93. MY GOALS ARE A PART OF WHAT I AM IN LIFE (p. 158)

Close your eyes. See yourself doing your life work and working on goals. See how you feel. Talk to yourself about how you feel. If you feel happy, calm, and joyous about your goals or your life work, just feel it. If you have worries, anxieties, or fears about your goals, just love the you you see inside and know that you have wisdom within to help you accomplish them. Listen very carefully to these concerns. Now relax and imagine yourself working or playing at fulfilling life tasks naturally and easily. See your life day by day as full of joy, love, and caring. See your work and goals flow out of the most creative, natural, and happy part of yourself.

94. HOW I WANT MY WORLD (p. 162)

Close your eyes. Imagine the world you want. Imagine how people will act toward each other. Imagine what you will be doing and how you will live and be with other people in this world. Imagine how all of the people in your world will be with each other. Imagine how the world will look and feel. How will you feel? When you have come back from the world you want, draw, write, or make up something about this vision.

95. I CAN BE HELPFUL (p. 163)

Think about helpful things you can do for others. Imagine yourself doing these things. How are they affecting the people? Does this affect other people that you are not directly helping? Do something helpful. See if it is like a stone thrown into the pond causing ripples moving outward. Notice if your being helpful inspires your friends to be helpful. See your helpful work going around the world.

INDEX

A, B

208

210

ABOUT THE AUTHOR

Claudia King is a native of California who wears many hats. Her primary allegiances being to beauty and love. She has been a teacher longer than a mother. Has studied and taught at several Universities, with Berkeley providing an early opening onto the universe. Claudia considers herself a creative artist with many approaches to creativity including painting and filmmaking as well as writing. Her children and grandchildren have taught her the importance of love as the only worthy power on the planet.

$ 6.94

LONGWOOD PUBLIC LIBRARY
800 Middle Country Road
Middle Island, NY 11953
(631) 924-6400
longwoodlibrary.org

LIBRARY HOURS

Monday-Friday	9:30 a.m. - 9:00 p.m.
Saturday	9:30 a.m. - 5:00 p.m.
Sunday (Sept-June)	1:00 p.m. - 5:00 p.m.